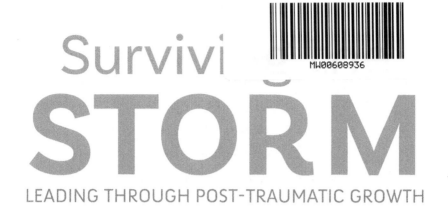

# Surviving STORM

## LEADING THROUGH POST-TRAUMATIC GROWTH

**LindaGail Walker**

*in collaboration with*
**REX MILLER**

[ME]Pub

Published by

[ME]Publishing

690 NE 23rd Ave, Gainesville, FL 32609

meteoreducationpublishing.com

[ME]Publishing

690 NE 23rd Ave, Gainesville, FL 32609

The advice and strategies found within may not be suitable for every situation.
This work is sold with the understanding that neither the author nor the
publisher are held responsible for the results accrued from the advice in this
book. Readers should be aware that Internet Web sites offered as citations and/
or sources for further information may have changed or disappeared between
the time this was written and when it is read.

Some names and identifying details have been changed to protect the privacy
of individuals. Stories within may sound like your story and probably are yours
and hundreds of others.

Cover image: Adobe Stock Images

Cover design: Joseph R. Myers

Layout: Marilee Pankratz

ISBN 978-1-7334334-4-0

Printed in the United States of America

# TABLE OF CONTENTS

For additional information and resources
scan the QR Code above.

# ACKNOWLEDGEMENTS

The influence of hundreds of educators and children has touched each and every page of this book. To try and name them all would be impossible, but their stories kept coming to the forefront of my mind as I went on this journey. This book is theirs as much as mine.

Without the support of my patient, loving, and thoughtful family, this book couldn't have come to life. They often heard during the process, "Just a second...I'm writing. Yes, still..." and made sure all my needs were met—including laughter! Their encouragement, support, and faith gave me the confidence to not only start this project but to continue on when I was unsure if I could.

I also thank the leaders and colleagues at Meteor Education for their confidence and conviction that this book would help our school communities as they move into uncharted waters. There are dozens of people who have significantly influenced this book and it would be impossible to mention each of them. However, I want to thank and acknowledge the contributions of the [ME]Pub staff and contractors who heroically brought it together. Thanks to the editorial staff—Sarah, Jennifer, and Andrew—for their keen eye, and desire to make my voice better. I thank the design staff, especially Marilee, for the pursuit of communicating how this book should "feel." And finally, thank you to Laura, my acquisitions editor, for her friendship, and to my publisher, Joseph, for his guidance. It's also important to recognize and thank Rex for collaborating on this project with me. Thank you also to Dr. Jernigan for your contribution.

# CHAPTER 1: DISRUPTED LIFE
## Thriving in a Storm of Trauma—Individually and Collectively

**M**elissa and Cindy are twins who have been through the storm. According to Melissa, "My mom loved us, but she loved meth and heroin more. To buy drugs, she made us do things that no little girls should do." They were finally removed from the home when a neighbor witnessed her mom's boyfriend knock Melissa across the yard as she tried to stop him from pulling Cindy inside. They never saw their mother again.

The twins settled into a foster home where they experienced consistent care they had never known before, yet they still missed their mother and hoped she would come to take them home again. Melissa remembers a watershed moment when Mrs. Mayo, her foster mother, sat the girls down and laid out a harsh truth: "Your mom is not coming back to get you. She signed away her rights. If you sit around here moping, you'll end up just like her. There is no one coming to rescue you girls. You have to do it yourselves. I am here to help you help yourselves." From that moment, Melissa and Cindy's lives diverged. Melissa threw herself into school and church under Mrs. Mayo's strict direction. After aging out of the foster care system at 18, she went on to college, became a second grade teacher, got married, and had a little girl of her own. Today she volunteers with a nonprofit that helps kids in foster care.

But what of Cindy? She ran away at 16 and was homeless. She moved in with someone who trafficked her to support a drug habit, and Cindy eventually went to jail for possession and prostitution. Melissa only heard from her when Cindy was in trouble and needed help, but no amount of money, advice, or love could bring peace to her turbulent life. Cindy lashed out at her sister the last time they met: "You think you're better than me now, but we were the same," Cindy told her sister. "We were the same for a long time." She was right. She and Melissa were the same for a long time. But not anymore.

The numbers aren't on the side of the nearly 500,000 children in foster care in the United States. According to the FBI, nearly 60% of child sex trafficking victims have spent time in foster care or group homes. Over 50% of foster care children experience serious mental health problems. Of the 26,000 youth who age out of the system every year, only 58% graduate high school; 50% are still unemployed by age 24, and 20% become homeless; 25% will be involved in the criminal justice system in their first two years after leaving foster care.[1]

But these brutal statistics are not the whole story. For all the "Cindys," there are also "Melissas" who are determined not to be victims and who find the resilience and resolve to save themselves. How does one person transform her life while another in the same circumstances stays stuck?

> How does one person transform her life while another in the same circumstance stays stuck?

## Our Generation's Storm

This is a question that should matter to all of us. Traumatized people experience great disruption to their sense of identity, significance, belonging, and hope. Even if we have not experienced trauma, we interact daily with those who do. Millions of people have experienced the trauma of physical, sexual, or emotional abuse, the loss of a loved one, a divorce, life-threatening accidents, or participating in war as a combatant or civilian. PTSD, a subset of trauma, will affect about 6% of the population at some point in their lives; in any given year about 15 million adults suffer with it.[2] A January 2021 study of the United States and four other Western countries found that 13% of people complained of PTSD symptoms related to the coronavirus and the measures put in place to control it. Interestingly, the study also showed that those symptoms were more intense in the anticipation of a negative experience than in the actual experience.[3]

Trauma can be collective as well as individual. In the past two years, trauma has increased 30% as we have experienced a "perfect storm" of disruptive events: a global pandemic along with lockdowns and new routines of work and education; volatile partisan divisions; economic recession; inflation; supply chain disruptions; racial tensions; mass protests; and an unsatisfying end to foreign wars that have cost us dearly in lives, treasure, and global influence. We've only begun to realize the educational toll all this will take. Social and emotional skills are learned during preschool; the window for reading skills is third grade, and math proficiency must be developed by fifth grade. We now have had two cohorts—some 60 million students— miss each window, increasing their risk of academic failure.[4] We will be dealing with the legacy of this setback for decades to come. All in all, we're facing a generation-defining existential crisis. How we come through it will shape the future of our children, our country, and the world.

So how are you and those in your orbit weathering this storm of a century? Many of the leaders I have worked with during the COVID-19 pandemic describe themselves as being in a state of "excited exhaustion," as if their minds are running in high gear all the time. This is what we call "survival brain." See if these aspects of living in survival brain sound familiar:

1. **Lack of focus:** fogginess, difficulty concentrating, trouble finishing an activity efficiently.
2. **Change in memory:** difficulty remembering details and daily events, confusion when trying to answer the question "How was your day?"
3. **Fatigue:** physical and mental exhaustion; going through your day like a sleepwalker.
4. **Emotional reactivity:** getting upset about things that normally wouldn't bother you, being snippy or grumpy with others, crying more easily.
5. **Neglecting basic needs:** letting housework pile up; forgetting to brush your teeth and wash your face; skipping your exercise routine.
6. **Impulsivity:** excessive spending or eating, trying activities that are uncharacteristic for you.

What about children? We see some of the same characteristics, but survival brain can look a little different for young people. Some signs that a child might be experiencing trauma include:

9

## SURVIVING THE STORM

1. **Emotional reactivity:** increased emotional dysregulation such as crying, yelling, or aggressive actions.

2. **Social withdrawal:** the child may stop doing activities that bring them joy and have difficulty engaging with others in conversation.

3. **Trust issues:** the child may have difficulty trusting others and may break trust through lying, stealing, or keeping secrets.

4. **Jumpiness:** being more reactive to stimuli, hyper-alert, and on edge.

5. **Zoning out:** losing focus, not hearing their name when called, being "in a different world."[5]

Do any of these aspects of survival brain remind you of yourself or members of your community? If so, this book is for you. Although the book is primarily addressed to educational professionals, its observations and suggestions will also be useful to parents, businesspeople, spiritual leaders—anyone who has the potential to be a positive and healing influence on traumatized people, especially students.

Maybe, on the other hand, you wonder what the fuss is about. Yes, we have been through some inconvenient disruptions, but you and your team are handling the crisis well. You feel calm, capable, and in control, and wonder why so many others seem to be struggling while you and your team make surfing the waves look easy. But even the most capable and optimistic people still struggle—sometimes intensely—without necessarily showing it, especially if they are part of a high-performing crew. Uncertainty, fear, and grief affect all of us. Just because someone appears to carry the weight better doesn't mean the weight is not heavy.

It's important even when things appear to be going swimmingly that leaders do not assume all is well, but create a culture of trust and transparency to make it safe for people to unburden themselves with others who can help share their emotional loads.

## Navigational Guides

The good news is that not only can we get through trauma to post-traumatic growth, but we can also begin to experience that growth during trauma. And we have scientific research that can help us find our way. Psychologist Martin Seligman conducted significant research in this field with returning soldiers from war in the Persian Gulf. Over 450,000 cases of post-traumatic stress disorder (PTSD) were diagnosed in returning soldiers—some 18% of the servicemen and women who completed tours of duty during the war. However, some came back stronger, through a resilient mindset, activating their strengths, relying on a circle of friends, managing their energy, finding a sense of purpose and meaning, and focusing on progress, not perfection.[6] The result? Post-traumatic growth.

Post-traumatic growth (PTG) is not simply casual terminology, but a theory developed by psychologists Richard Tedeschi and Lawrence Calhoun in the 1990s to explain why some people experience positive growth after trauma. As Dr. Tedeschi explains, through PTG, "People develop new understandings of themselves, the world they live in, how to relate to other people, the kind of future they might have, and a better understanding of how to live life."[7] Drs. Tedeschi and Calhoun developed the Post-Traumatic Growth Inventory (PTGI), a self-report scale that measures positive responses in five domains of post-traumatic growth:

- Appreciation of life
- Relationships with others
- New possibilities in life
- Personal strength
- Spiritual change

An estimated one-half to two-thirds of people who endure trauma eventually manifest one or more of these areas of PTG. Follow-up studies with family and friends of trauma victims show that this growth remains relatively stable over time. Those who have the most success are extroverts, who tend to have an openness to experience; women; and those in late adolescence and early adulthood. Genetic components may also play a role, but the science is not yet determinative on this question.[8]

Several of these factors applied to Melissa and her sister, but they weren't the whole story. To attribute Melissa's success to influences entirely outside of her control underestimates the tremendous amount of work it took to get where she is today. I talked with Mrs. Mayo about her experience with the twins. She said that for the first three months, the girls sat on the porch every day after school and waited, hoping their birth mother would come to take them home. The caseworker visits were heartbreaking because they would cry for days after their mom didn't show up. Both girls had night terrors about bogeymen that were all too real. Both had attachment issues after having learned to protect themselves just to survive. But when she talked to the girls about the reality of their situation, Mrs. Mayo unknowingly used the four key factors a leader can leverage to lead to post-traumatic growth:

- **Brutally honest optimism:** "No one is coming to save you, but I will help you."
- **Perceptions of control:** "Girls, you have to save yourselves."
- **Conveying coping mechanisms:** "If you sit around here moping, it won't help."
- **Instilling a strong sense of self:** "I am here to help you help yourselves."

In subsequent work with Melissa and Cindy over the years, Mrs. Mayo built upon this foundation with scaffolded skills, support, and empowerment for the girls to experience post-traumatic growth.

No matter how resilient a person is, there is no guarantee they will beat the odds and escape psychological damage from severe trauma. Experiencing trauma challenges core beliefs, creates intense psychological struggle, and requires that we find our way through it to personal growth.[9] Post-traumatic growth takes time, energy, and struggle. It is not a quick fix. It may come with some stumbles. And as Cindy's story illustrates, not everyone will respond in the same way or with the same degree of success. However, it's also not just a matter of luck. The odds of success are greatly improved when there is a leader present who takes timely and appropriate action to help these skills flourish. Leaders can't ensure that others will grow, but they, just like Mrs. Mayo, can lay a foundation and provide an environment that makes growth possible.

## Take the Wheel
Are you that kind of leader? Maybe you don't feel like it, but odds are, you're already doing the job without realizing it. This is certainly a time that calls for the best leadership we can muster. Yet even in the best of times, leading is hard. Pick your metaphor: herding cats, putting out fires. Leadership is often an extended exercise in crisis management. Maybe right now it feels like herding cats while putting out fires . . . in a hurricane. As a leader, it's not enough to hold yourself together; you must direct an exhausted and (sometimes literally) sick crew trying to navigate in completely uncharted waters. You're throwing out life preservers to everyone else while weathering your own traumas, personally and

professionally. You're staying afloat for now. But are you even going in the right direction?

Take heart. You're probably doing better than you realize. Having witnessed her fair share of storms living in the prairies of Nebraska, the great novelist Willa Cather observed, "There are some things you learn best in calm, and some in storm."[10] Something we've learned in our current storm is that leaders rise to the occasion when they are needed, sometimes filling roles they never expected, but doing whatever is necessary to get the job done. Unlike the movies, where one hero saves the day virtually single-handedly, in real life it takes whole communities deliberately putting one foot in front of the other, day in and day out. And real-life heroes usually see their own heroism as just part of the job, rather than the extraordinarily courageous leadership it is.

> "There are some things you learn best in calm, and some in storm." – Willa Cather

No matter how much we may feel fear and uncertainty, and mourn the tragic casualties of the storm, these things don't have to define us. We can create—and live—a narrative built around everyday examples of people serving with humanity, humility, and heroism. As Fred Rogers famously recalled,

> When I was a boy and I would see scary things in the news, my mother would say to me, "Look for the helpers. You will always find people who are helping." To this day, especially in times of "disaster," I remember my mother's words and I am always comforted by realizing that there are still so many helpers – so many caring people in this world.[11]

This is true of people making vital, constructive contributions in all fields: from first responders to front-line medical workers, the military, and even our local food service workers. But perhaps no public servants are as well-positioned to shape the resilience and leadership potential of the next generation as educational professionals.

## SURVIVING THE STORM

As an educator, you already have experience leading others through trauma. Researchers Lea Waters and Tom Brunzell note that even in "normal" times some 40% of U.S. students have been exposed to traumatic stressors such as sexual or physical assault or witnessing domestic violence. These traumatic experiences can produce mental states of grief, abandonment, anxiety, fear, and depression. For many students, school is a safe haven where they can form relationships, feel connected to stable and consistent authority figures, and experience success in challenging but manageable daily tasks. To help students manage their trauma responses, teachers can use specific techniques such as facilitating positive relationships, creating a positive physical space for learning, priming students to experience positive emotions, helping students recognize and develop their character strengths, and building resilience skills.[12]

## TEACHING TECHNIQUES FOR TRAUMA[13]

Lea Waters and Tom Brunzell offer the following teaching techniques that can help trauma-affected students, and are also great for students who aren't currently suffering from trauma. How many of these are you already using? Which one could you most easily integrate into your current classroom culture?

1. **POSITIVE RELATIONSHIPS** – building relational trust with authority figures by smiling, getting to know students as individuals, sharing parts of your life, and modeling reliable and regulated adult behavior.

2. **POSITIVE PHYSICAL SPACE** – using lighting, decorations, plants, and furniture arrangements to create a sense of safety. Creating a mindfulness corner with beanbags, squeeze toys, coloring books, and other stress-relieving activities.

3. **POSITIVE PRIMING** – using escalating brain breaks to build positive energy (clapping, thumb wars, races) and de-escalating brain breaks to build calm emotions (silently tracing the movements of a partner, playing music, body movements such as shrugging or pumping one's toes).

4. **USING CHARACTER STRENGTHS** – identifying strengths with surveys, strengths cards, and strength-spotting exercises. Discussing character traits of literary or historical figures. Developing strengths through the performing arts, sports, and other co-curricula.

5. **BUILDING RESILIENCE** – role playing skills such as setting boundaries and verbalizing feelings in the safety of the classroom. Using negative self-talk as a teachable moment to suggest positive alternatives (I can't do this = Maybe I'm tired and need a break).

## SURVIVING THE STORM

Even in the absence of specific training in trauma-informed learning, many excellent teachers are already instinctively managing their students in ways that make school not only an educational experience, but a psychologically healing one as well. However, given the overwhelming circumstances in which we find ourselves, we cannot take it for granted that effectual learning and recovery will happen without forethought or effort. A critical first step is to understand the typical phases of trauma we go through during a mass disaster event, at both an individual and a societal level.

## Mapping a Mental Health Disaster

The uneasy sense of sailing in uncharted waters makes a crisis feel ten times worse. We can gain some navigational clues, though, from the typical behavioral health symptoms people display during traumatic events. The chart below is adapted from The Substance Abuse and Mental Health Services Administration (SAMHSA), an agency of the U.S. Department of Health and Human Services charged with reducing the impact of substance abuse and mental illness on America's communities. It illustrates the relationship between traumatic events and our emotional states. A practical application of this emotional "map" is to help leaders be proactive in communication, preparing those under their leadership for emotional lows and building relational collateral during emotional highs.

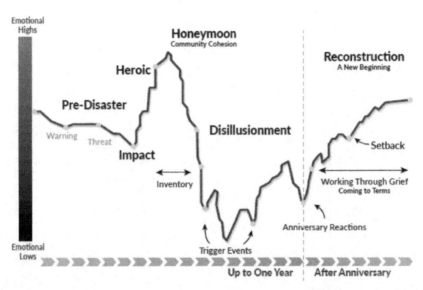

From *Strategy in Rebuilding* by Rex Miller and Jeff Jernigan; graph adapted from *The Substance Abuse and Mental Health Services Administration*

Let's take a deeper dive into each of these phases. Suggestions for application and reflection prompts in each section below can help educational leaders contemplate what phase they are in and how best to help their community navigate the stages ahead.

## PHASE 1: PRE-DISASTER

The pre-disaster phase is characterized by fear and uncertainty. Disasters that occur with no warning can result in feelings of vulnerability and a lack of security, fears of the future and unpredicted tragedies, and a sense of loss of control or inability to protect oneself and one's family. On the other hand, disasters that come with warnings can cause guilt or self-blame for failure to heed those warnings. The pre-disaster phase may be as short as hours or even minutes, such as during a terrorist attack. Alternatively, it may be several months, such as during a hurricane season.

As we first began to hear about the new coronavirus, few realized the sudden and lasting implications it would have on schools and communities. I had scheduled a trip for mid-March 2020 to visit a school in Westchester County, New York, one of the first hot spots of COVID. Two weeks before the trip, everything was fine. Five days later, their world had changed. Store shelves were empty, businesses had shut down, and school closures were imminent. In a few short weeks the entire nation would be in various stages of lockdown. Our on-site visit didn't happen until 18 months down the road.

**Phase 1 Suggestions:** Be visible and present. Provide reassurance that you see the potential threat and take it seriously. Explain how you will monitor, prepare, and keep people informed. Let people know how they can prepare for the impact and aftermath of the disaster.

**Phase 1 Reflection:** Think back to the first time you heard of COVID-19. Did you believe that it might directly impact you and your school community? Knowing what you know now, what are ways you might have prepared for the disaster differently?

## PHASE 2: IMPACT

The impact phase is usually the shortest of the six stages of a disaster. In this stage, we weather a range of intense emotional reactions. Initial confusion and disbelief are typically followed by a focus on self-preservation and family protection.

## SURVIVING THE STORM

When the pandemic began in 2020, school communities across the nation quickly shifted to alternative avenues of instruction, whether online or by means of paper packets so that students without access to technology would not miss instruction. Many of us thought things would go "back to normal" soon, but they didn't. The unpredictability of the virus itself fueled fear: Some people got infected but were asymptomatic; others had a couple of days of flu-like symptoms; others required hospitalization and struggled with long-term medical issues; and tragically, many of the most vulnerable lost their lives. Fear of the unknown fueled irrational panic buying, the spreading of rumors, and a search for reliable information. Combating the virus with social isolation exacerbated its mental health effects as well as its economic and social impact. Families hunkered down in metaphorical "bubbles," giving themselves some feeling of security by applying hand sanitizer and counting their rolls of toilet paper.

**Phase 2 Suggestions:** Your school community should have an emergency response team and process. In the impact stage of a disaster, they should initially focus on assessing the effects of the situation on students and teachers. Contingency planning should have a triage model for response and for supporting members of the school community at different levels of impact. It's important to remember that emergency response team members also have personal and family needs that must be attended to during the crisis.

**Phase 2 Reflection:** How did the initial stages of the pandemic affect your daily life and your emotional state? How well was your leadership team able to recognize and respond supportively to signs of stress in your school community?

## PHASE 3: THE HEROIC PHASE

The heroic phase is characterized by a high level of activity with a low level of productivity. During this phase, employees and the public display a sense of altruism, and many community members exhibit adrenaline-induced rescue behavior. Heroic efforts may impair full risk assessment. The heroic phase often passes quickly into phase 4.

In the heroic phase of the pandemic many school boards moved rapidly to help students and the community. States lifted standardized testing requirements. Teachers quickly learned unfamiliar technology and teaching methods. School leaders made plans to ensure that the most vulnerable had food and shelter. Administrators put effort and creativity into creating meaningful and memorable online or drive-through graduations. All of this extra effort came in the context of most employees working from home, with dual responsibilities as caregivers to their own children. At this stage of the crisis, many people—though not all—practiced greater patience, were creative about checking in with others, and were increasingly aware of the importance of mental well-being.

**Phase 3 Suggestions:** Seeing the high levels of altruism, community spirit, and activity during this period, it's tempting to set goals that will turn out to be unsustainable in the long run. It's important that we don't misread short-term responses as long-term potential. To avoid fatigue in this temporary adrenaline-fueled phase, school leaders will want to model a healthy balance between working hard and practicing self-care under highly demanding conditions. Wise leaders will recognize the need to reestablish a realistic pace and support their employees in creating a healthy work/life balance.

The high level of activity in this phase can be a form of self-medication for the deep anxiety the crisis is causing. Providing thoughtful responses to concerns without using fear-based language can go a long way to calming frayed nerves. A consistent, disciplined response to new developments during the crisis might include:

- "This is what we know."
- "This is what we are looking into."
- "Here are some sources you might find helpful in answering your questions."
- "Please share your questions and concerns and we will work to find a solution."
- "Circumstances will often change until things stabilize. We will regularly share what we know and what we are learning."

**Phase 3 Reflection:** How have you seen heroic acts come to life in your school community? What is sustainable and what needs to be let go? How can you celebrate acts of heroism from your staff?

### PHASE 4: HONEYMOON

A dramatic shift in emotion happens during the honeymoon phase. As disaster assistance is made available, optimism rises and the community bonds. People think they see light at the end of the tunnel and assume the worst of the disaster is behind them. However, the honeymoon phase is only an interim period of weeks to a few months. It's like the calm eye of a hurricane—merely a pause until the next phase hits.

If school administrators don't read this period correctly, they may begin setting plans and timelines for recovery too soon, only to frustrate staff, students, and parents when events suddenly worsen, requiring that those decisions be walked back. The honeymoon phase is a great time to build trust and bond with staff members, reaching out as needed and encouraging everyone to take advantage of the pause to practice healthy self-care. When the next stage begins, the connections created during this phase will be critical to the school community.

**Phase 4 Suggestions:** This is perhaps the most crucial period to the morale of your organization. It's a welcome reprieve that allows everyone to take a breath, bond, and celebrate wins. Being too upbeat about every positive trend will be harmful in the long-run, though, because it will lead to breaking trust and deepening disillusionment when future challenges emerge. Your team should celebrate wins, but they should be placed in the context of the events of recent history and a realistic estimation of future potential.

**Phase 4 Reflection:** How have you felt when overly-optimistic projections about COVID-19 turned out to be unrealistic? What are some specific ways you can bond with your team during the honeymoon period to prepare for the challenges ahead?

### PHASE 5: DISILLUSIONMENT

In stark contrast to the honeymoon phase, the disillusionment phase signals that the population's limits of endurance are being reached. Further disaster assistance is not forthcoming. Setbacks have occurred in the unrealistic plans that were made in earlier stages. Inconsistent official statements and gaps in disaster assistance have undermined confidence in our institutions' ability to cope with the conditions. As discouragement sets in, attitudes shift from "we're in this together" to "every person for themselves." Workers and students become disengaged and apathetic. Some will begin to manifest unhealthy behaviors such as substance abuse, domestic violence, protests, acts of resistance, and even sabotage, riots, or other violence.

The breach of trust in authority produces hyper-vigilance that may be projected toward school employees and leaders, resulting in unruly behavior at school board meetings, resistance to school policies, confrontational attitudes toward teachers and administrators, and even threats of violence. Unfortunately, the disillusionment phase can last months and even years. One or a series of trigger events can quickly set back hard-won progress.

**Phase 5 Suggestions:** At this stage, transparency can be helpful in rebuilding trust. Be willing to acknowledge what has gone well, what hasn't, and what you're doing about it. It's also an important time for collaborative conversations and listening to disparate opinions, even those that may be heavily weighted with misplaced emotion. Allowing people to vent can be a healing activity, especially if we can walk them back from "us vs. them" thinking. This is a great time to check in with team members in a personalized way: a phone call, a handwritten note, grabbing coffee together (in virtual space if necessary). Weary and disillusioned people appreciate knowing they are not alone.

**Phase 5 Reflection:** How can you increase transparency and clear communication with your constituents and your campus or district leadership? In this stage, how have your values, vision, and mission held up? What changes may need to occur?

## PHASE 6: RECONSTRUCTION AND REFORM

An overall feeling of recovery is the norm during the reconstruction phase. Individuals and communities begin to assume responsibility for rebuilding their lives. People adjust to a "new normal" while continuing to grieve losses—especially lost loved ones, but also skipped holidays and milestones such as graduations and weddings, the aftermath of job loss and financial setbacks, and hundreds of plans and dreams, large and small, irrevocably impacted by a catastrophic event. The reconstruction phase often starts around the anniversary of the disaster and may continue for months or years depending upon the scope of the losses and the necessary material and emotional recovery.

**Phase 6 Suggestions:** During this phase, your school community will likely make several fundamental shifts in strategic direction. Decisions will need to be made about the future role of online learning, for example, along with adjustments to technology investment and training. Every disaster requires a reassessment of emergency response protocols to correct deficiencies, improve effectiveness, and shorten response times in future contingencies. Staffing levels and assignments may need to be adjusted, and the efficacy of allowing some staff to continue working from home needs to be considered. Each of these decisions will contend with legacy behaviors, a fall in performance during the learning curve, and competition between various internal interests.

**Phase 6 Reflection:** What strengths have you observed in your school community during the crisis? How can your team capitalize on these by working smarter, not harder? What are the possibilities for incremental improvements that will be manageable and motivational to an exhausted staff?

## Now What?

I worked intensely with Amy, a district leader, to customize a leadership academy for her district. As we discussed the effects of trauma, stress, and learning gaps exacerbated by the pandemic, she said, "Well, thank you so much for all of that information. It is devastating and we aren't prepared so now what?" We've started assessing the problem, but what we can do about it?

My intention in this book is to, first, raise awareness of the dimensions of the mental health crisis we are facing. The extent of this crisis may be underestimated and will certainly last long after the resolution of the immediate public health crisis posed by COVID-19. To that end, each chapter of this book focuses on a significant area of traumatic disruption of our lives and relationships. Sidebars, pull quotes, feature articles, and discussion questions at the end of each chapter, based on the five domains of post-traumatic growth, will offer useful prompts for meaningful conversations with your coworkers and constituents. My aim is not just to provide you with esoteric information, but actionable knowledge that can improve your performance and that of your team during and after a traumatic event.

There will be an ebb and a flow to this storm, and that is exhausting in and of itself. Even when it eventually passes, there will be other storms ahead. No one specific crisis is the sum of the problem, whether it's COVID-19, political partisanship, globalization, or any of the other myriad dilemmas currently challenging us. The problem is learning to live in a world where chaos is always ready to overtake the order we try to create, like waves eroding sandcastles on the seashore. The pandemic is a tsunami, no doubt about it, but it is also part of an endless procession of waves, large and small. We can't stop the waves, but we can learn to ride them. My hope is the lessons we are learning together about post-traumatic growth during the present crisis will better equip us and our children to grow, not only after future crises pass, but as we live through them.

A key learning from this book is that your leadership through post-traumatic growth will impact your entire community in a way that not only helps them survive but thrive. You don't have to be a "born leader." The kind of leadership we need is built through daily interactions, practices, and habits, modeled by a few, appreciated and emulated by many. In the end, it won't be spectacular, attention-grabbing headlines people will remember. It will be the small things that give them hope in their darkest moments. The storm doesn't have to define us . . . but our reaction to it might.

> The storm doesn't have to define us . . . but our reaction to it might.

## SURVIVING THE STORM

### REFLECTION QUESTIONS

1. Which character in the stories of the foster children do you most identify with? What do you find encouraging or challenging about that similarity?

2. Which of the five domains of post-traumatic growth have you noticed in yourself and your colleagues? How can you build on that new growth?

3. Which phase of the crisis do you think you and your organization are in at the moment? What are you doing well, and what do you need to improve to lead well at this phase?

### STRAIGHTFORWARD SURVIVAL

When we experience disruption, sometimes we need simple ideas for taking a next, practical step forward. If you are unsure of where to start, choose one of these ideas from the chapter:

- Create small wins and celebrations. What has gone well lately?

- Reflect on what you can control and influence.

- Reframe challenges into chances to develop, learn, and grow your agility. What recent problem can you start to look at as an opportunity?

## ENDNOTES

1.  Mission & Stats. Foundation for Foster Children. (n.d.). Retrieved February 2, 2022, from https://foundationforfosterchildren.org/who-we-are/mission-stats/

2.  Va.gov: Veterans Affairs. How Common is PTSD in Adults? (2018, September 13). Retrieved April 4, 2022, from https://www.ptsd.va.gov/understand/common/common_adults.asp.

3.  M. Iati, (2021, December 25), "The Pandemic Has Caused Nearly Two Years of Collective Trauma." *The Washington Post*. Retrieved April 4, 2022, from https://www.washingtonpost.com/health/2021/12/24/collective-trauma-public-out-bursts/.

4.  R. Miller (personal communication, March 8, 2022).

5.  "Trauma and the Brain: Signs You Might be Living in 'Survival Mode,'" (2021, January 4). Child Guidance. Retrieved February 3, 2022, from https://cgrc.org/blog/trauma-and-the-brain-signs-you-might-be-in-survival-mode/.

6.  R. Miller (2021, June 14), "Thriving in All Seasons: The 6 Disciplines to Post-traumatic Growth." Retrieved February 9, 2022, from https://www.youtube.com/watch?v=X9aUzP3cook&t=17s.

7.  L. Collier, (2016, November), "Growth After Trauma," *Monitor on Psychology*. Retrieved February 8, 2022, from https://www.apa.org/monitor/2016/11/growth-trauma.

8.  Collier, L. (2016, November). Growth after trauma. Monitor on Psychology. Retrieved February 8, 2022, from https://www.apa.org/monitor/2016/11/growth-trauma.

9.  "Trauma and Shock," (n.d.), American Psychological Association, Retrieved February 8, 2022, from https://www.apa.org/topics/trauma.

10. W. Cather. (1915). *The Song of the Lark*. Boston: Houghton Mifflin.

11. A. Harris, (2013, April 16), "The History of Mister Rogers' Powerful Message," *Slate Magazine*. Retrieved February 8, 2022 from https://slate.com/culture/2013/04/look-for-the-helpers-mister-rogers-quote-a-brief-history.html.

12. "Five Ways to Support Students Affected by Trauma," (2018), *Greater Good Magazine*. Retrieved from https://greatergood.berkeley.edu/article/item/five_ways_to_support_ students_affected_by_trauma.

13. Ibid.

14. R. Miller and J. Jernigan. *Strategy in Rebuilding: Principles to Building Post-traumatic Growth*. https://rexmiller.com/shop/ols/products/strategy-in-rebuilding-principles-to-build-post-traumatic-growth-str-in-rbl-prn1.

# CHAPTER 2: RESTORING CAPACITY
## Restoring Function in Times of Grief and Trauma

Amelia Vanek, the heroine of the 2014 film *The Babadook*, is a single mom who lost her husband in a car accident. She's doing her best to cope, but as her son Sam's behavioral issues escalate, she feels her sanity slipping. Then comes Mister Babadook. No one knows exactly what the Babadook is or where it came from. At first it's just a disturbing character in a creepy children's book. But soon it's clear that it has a life and a will of its own. It intrudes into Amelia's world as a dark, shadowy, unnaturally tall apparition, a menacing figure just outside the field of peripheral vision. Amelia tries to ignore it, to push it out of her mind, but it hisses at her, "The more you deny the stronger I get." Finally facing the creature, Amelia manages to force it into the basement, where she can keep it contained . . . but for how long?

So what is Mister Babadook? Film critic Wael Khairy suggests,

> The malevolent Babadook is basically a physicalised form of the mother's trauma . . . The Babadook embodies the destructive power of grief. Throughout the film, we see the mother insist nobody bring up her husband's name. She basically lives in denial. Amelia has repressed grief for years, refusing to surrender to it.[1]

Amelia's unaddressed grief diminishes her capacity to think clearly, to earn a living, to give her son the support and psychological help he needs. It damages her relationship with her son's teachers, her sister, and others who try to help. Yet for most of the film she misses the signs, doesn't see the significance of what is happening, and doesn't realize that working through her own trauma will be the key to resolving the overwhelming and immediate problems of her life. Her capacity must be restored if she is to face these challenges. For us, as for Amelia, a critical first step in restoring disrupted capacity is to face the demons of our own traumatic grief.

## Hurricane or Tsunami?

Grief and trauma are similar, but not identical. Grief is a hurricane. Trauma is a tsunami. The comparison can take us only so far, but these are memorable images that can help us understand how mass disaster events may short-circuit the expected grieving processes and diminish our capacity to function and move into post-traumatic growth.

> Grief is a hurricane. Trauma is a tsunami.

2021 was one of the most active hurricane seasons in U.S. history, with 21 named storms causing $70 billion in damages and killing more than 160 people.[2] As terrible as they are, hurricanes have one thing in their favor: *We know when they are coming.* Satellites track them as they form thousands of miles away. Weather services predict where they are likely to make landfall, allowing states to issue evacuation orders to minimize loss of life.

Tsunamis often strike without warning. On December 26, 2004, a magnitude 9.1 earthquake lifted the ocean floor off Sumatra 130 feet, triggering 100-foot high waves that crashed into the city of Banda Aceh, killing more than 100,000 people. By the time the wave swept across the Indian Ocean, some 230,000 people had died.[3] Without warning, unseen forces twisted a perfectly normal day into a chaotic fight for survival.

Like a hurricane, grief is disruptive and devastating, but often we can see it coming and prepare for it. After my aging father was diagnosed with a degenerative terminal illness, our family had seven long years to wrap our minds around losing him. Others might see a divorce or job loss coming months in advance. Any significant loss that an individual experiences as a disruption of their quest for identity, significance, belonging, and hope can elicit a grief response.  Grief is never easy. We experience it and process it in different ways. Generally, though, we get through it, recover our capacity to function, and move on.

Trauma is a tsunami. One minute we're living our lives, the next a shocking loss hits and we're struggling just to stay on our feet. Any event that threatens our life or the lives of those we care about—whether we experience it, witness it, or even just become aware of it—can create feelings of helplessness, fear, or horror.[4] War, abuse, a car accident, the unexpected death of a loved one—all of these can be traumatic, and even create secondary trauma for first responders and others who hear of the event or see images of it in the media. Noting the ubiquity of trauma experiences, Doni Wilson remarks, "We all have a sea of troubles at some point in our lives. Some of us just have bigger monsters in our particular sea."[5]

COVID-19 brought a lot of monsters to a lot of seas. People lost loved ones, jobs, businesses, and homes, and missed graduations, birthdays, weddings, and the births of grandchildren. In ordinary times, such losses would happen over the course of years and individuals would move through a grieving process at their own pace with the help of their community. However, the circumstances of lockdown short-circuited our regular rituals of mourning and comforting one another. People died alone due to hospital visitation restrictions. Funerals and church services became virtual affairs, lacking all-important human contact. Pandemic news, store signs, and mask-covered faces acted as daily triggers stoking emotional responses. Through it all many people became stuck in various stages of grief, unable to recover their disrupted capacity and move forward to post-traumatic growth.[6]

## Grief Stories We Tell Ourselves
Given that grief is a pervasive human experience, how do we get through the disruption this hurricane brings to our lives? Psychiatrist Elisabeth Kübler-Ross proposed a five-phase model that has become a standard in discussions of grief. Her research was specific to death and dying, so the model may not fit other contexts exactly. However, many people find her framework helpful in navigating other kinds of devastating losses.

Each person responds to grief in individual ways. Grieving does not always proceed in a linear fashion through the stages, nor is it completed all at once and left behind. Grieving people may cycle through different stages out of order, move through them multiple times even in the same day, or get stuck in one stage for a long time. Well after it seems the grieving process is done, a triggering event may return a person to one or more stages of grief that need to be worked through for deeper healing.

To move away from the notion that grieving is a linear process, I'd like to suggest we view the stages of grief as five stories we tell ourselves to try to make sense of what has happened. When faced with new information that doesn't make sense to us, we try to organize it into a more coherent narrative to reduce our anxiety.[7] Becoming aware of the patterns of these stories can help us work through our own grieving process, and it can help us consider how we might respond in a more helpful and healing way when we see grief-driven behaviors in others.

### The Kübler–Ross Change Curve

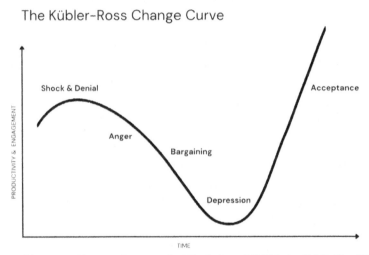

*"The Kübler-Ross Change Curve in the Workplace," (2022, April 11), The Whatfix Blog. Whatfix. Retrieved April 14, 2022, from https://whatfix.com/blog/kubler-ross-change-curve/*

### STORY 1: DENIAL

In denial, we protect ourselves by convincing ourselves the event is not that bad, or even that it never happened at all. A grieving person in denial may feel disconnected from reality and refuse to talk or even think about their loss.[8] They may neglect essential responsibilities, such as making funeral arrangements or filing insurance paperwork. Denial can serve a valid function to prepare us for emotional detachment, giving us a chance to experience a feeling of normalcy as we steel ourselves for the hard work of facing a loss. It becomes dysfunctional when we try to use it as a long-term coping strategy divorced from reality.

One of the most poignant stories that emerged from the Syrian civil war was that of a caring young father named Abdullah al-Mohammed, who taught his three-year-old daughter, Salwa, to laugh at the sound of explosions rather than fear them.[9] He used denial protectively, to tell his vulnerable child a story that was less frightening than reality. Sometimes we protect our "inner child" in the same way.

**Story 1 Suggestions:** In denial, individuals may resist making necessary plans, yet they are often willing to reminisce about pleasant times before the tragedy happened. We can help those who are grieving by providing a support network, listening to their memories, and helping them think about what is most important to them going forward.[10] In mass disasters, school administrators can provide opportunities for employees, students, and parents to celebrate memories of the school community before the disaster.

Fast-moving events require triage and timely action, so we do need to move forward with planning even during the denial stage. In the event of a death, the necessity of making funeral arrangements can help move survivors beyond denial. In the school environment, we can assign responsible parties to gather information and prepare contingency plans for alternative scenarios. These concrete organizational tasks can give team members a sense of control in an uncertain environment. In these tasks, individuals can model calm, matter-of-fact behavior to help each other feel safe without escaping into a fantasy that everything will be "back to normal" soon.

## STORY 2: ANGER

When reality can no longer be denied, a grief-stricken person may respond to a flood of painful emotions with a new story in which a villain has done them a great, unfair injustice. The villain might be medical personnel, politicians, or God. They might feel anger at a deceased loved one for leaving them. They might vent rage at friends and family, complete strangers, or inanimate objects. There is little use reasoning with a person in this painful emotional state; they likely already understand that their reaction is illogical, but that doesn't make it any easier to control their overwhelming feelings.[11]

## SURVIVING THE STORM

In a "normal" year, the Federal Aviation Administration investigates 150-200 unruly passenger incidents. In 2021 that figure rose to an astounding 5,981 incidents, an increase of approximately 3,000 percent.[12] One American Airlines passenger faced criminal prosecution after punching a female flight attendant in the face. Her offense? Accidentally bumping him—and apologizing for it—as she moved through the first-class cabin.[13] It's not hard to picture these types of reactions as extreme manifestations of grief at the losses, tension, and frustration of that year of the pandemic.

In the counseling field, anger is considered to be a "secondary" emotion that masks something deeper: sadness, shame, fear, etc. Whether we feel it ourselves or witness it in another, one of the first questions to ask is, "What lies underneath this?" Scratch a little beneath the surface of anger and you'll often find thinly-veiled grief.

**Story 2 Suggestions:** Anger from a student, parent, or coworker can easily trigger the same reaction in us, especially if we too are grieving in a mass disaster situation. As professionals, we can stay calm, de-escalate, and choose the time and manner of our response to the incident. One of the best ways to handle an emotional exchange is to validate the person's feelings—"I know we're all struggling right now and it's been a long day"—and then take a break: "Can we revisit this tomorrow after we've had some time to think about it?" We can also encourage those in our orbit to release angry feelings appropriately, such as through physical or creative activity. If there is legitimate concern that the person may harm themselves or others, professional help should of course be sought.[14]

### STORY 3: BARGAINING

When a person creates "bargaining" storylines, it's a sign of movement toward acceptance of their situation. They're willing to concede the outcome, yet still hold onto a thread of hope that it will somehow turn out differently. A dying person may try to give up smoking or eat a better diet to extend their life. Religious people may make promises to their higher power, hoping for a miraculous intervention. After a tragedy, those in grief might fantasize about how things would have turned out better if they had made different choices. Even though this "bargain" cannot be carried out, a grieving person can feel some sense of control in knowing the wise and effective thing they would choose to do if they could.[15] Some of the bargains we attempt to strike have nothing to do with the event itself. We might try to overperform in small, inconsequential things, like answering emails, redecorating our home office, or mastering the art of baking, as if these can change our situation.

When we try to reshape our story with "bargains," we might emerge from a crisis with a new skill, a cleaner house, and better exercise habits, yet none of that will restore the losses we have endured or take us all the way to the end of our grief journey. At some point, we have to face the unavoidable reality of what we experienced and acknowledge that our life will be different going forward.

**Story 3 Suggestions:** As we bring our bargaining storytelling to a close, it's reasonable to reevaluate the opportunity cost of some of the bargains we have struck. Are the new things we've added to our routines sustainable and useful going forward? We may have thought that closing schools for a year and switching to online learning were temporary concessions during the pandemic until everything could go back to normal. But as the social and psychological problems compound, academic performance drops, and overstretched teachers begin to change careers in record numbers, we have to face the fact that there will be no returning to the way things were. It's time to reframe the pandemic from a crisis to an *opportunity* to re-envision the way we do education.

### STORY 4: DEPRESSION

When the future a person previously imagined for themselves has collapsed, they may default to a story of depression. Overwhelmed with sadness, they feel defeated, drained of energy, unable to fight or bargain anymore. The outcome seems inevitable, and the only thing that can be done is to allow the waves of grief to roll over them. They may become silent and reclusive, spend long hours ruminating, and seem apathetic about life. Depression can be alarming to loved ones, who may misguidedly think their job is to "cheer them up" so they can "snap out of it." It's critical to remember that depression is a natural reaction to overwhelming loss, and that it helps people begin transitioning toward acceptance of the new situation.[16] Rushing a grieving person through this chapter of their story without fully understanding and experiencing it can leave them with unfinished psychological business that will continue to create problems for them in the future.

Jennifer lost her spouse in a car accident. She tried to bury the grief by returning quickly to her job as a school leader, but within months her untended depression affected the entire campus. Emails went unanswered.

Meetings lacked direction. Longstanding traditions were forgotten or delayed indefinitely. Jennifer simply didn't have the bandwidth to function while deeply mired in this stage of grief. Fortunately, the leadership team recognized what was happening and was able to fill in the gaps as she journeyed through this season until she was able to return to full capacity.

**Story 4 Suggestions:** The length of time a person will linger in a story of depression depends on many factors, including their relationship to the deceased or level of involvement in the crisis event, the time of year the loss took place (for example, around a holiday), and their own personality characteristics. Depressed people often choose to isolate themselves from their support networks. It's necessary to give them some space, but we must also be strategically present to let them know they are not alone and to help them reconnect with activities and people as they become able. Professional help may be necessary, especially if depression seems especially deep and long-lasting.

Educational settings can perform a necessary service by becoming true communities whose members know one another and feel safe confiding in one another when things are not going well. Some people are more high-functioning in their depression than others and will be able to hide it for quite some time in a busy workplace where people are not attuned to one another's emotions. In fact, putting on an unnaturally happy face in the presence of others can itself be a sign of depression.[17] Schools should take care to provide ways to involve students, faculty, and staff in small, safe groups where no one can get lost in the crowd, where everyone can tell their story to attentive, understanding ears, and where people ask questions to find out whether we're smiling or crying behind our masks.

**HIDDEN SIGNS OF DEPRESSION**[18]
Depression isn't always obvious. Review this list of hidden signs of depression. Who is the first person who comes to mind when you read this list? Should you reach out to see if they need help?

- Appetite and weight changes

- Changes in sleep habits

- Increased alcohol or drug use

- Fatigue

- Forced happiness

- Pessimism

- Loss of concentration

- Disinterest in hobbies

- Physical pains and health disorders

- Anger and irritability

- Low sex drive

## STORY 5: ACCEPTANCE

We can think of acceptance as the target story we're trying to construct. At this point, we're ready to build a satisfying story that lets us move on. This stage brings some emotional detachment and objectivity. We stop trying to get back to a lost "normal." We reconcile with the loss. We put one foot in front of the other and realize we can keep on doing that, every day, for a long time.

Acceptance doesn't mean we feel good about the loss, and it doesn't mean we forget about it, or the good times that came before. We regret what we've lost and we treasure our good memories. But acceptance is a decision to live in the present, acknowledging that the loss happened, that there is no going back, and that our lives going forward will be different. Acceptance turns our attention to the future. We set goals, do what is necessary to reach them, and celebrate our successes. New roles and relationships are developed, and we discover that joy can be part of our lives again.[19]

Some people experience guilt as they begin feeling purposeful and content again. It can feel like betrayal of what they have lost, especially if others have not reached this point in their grieving process. We do have to be sensitive to others' feelings, and we have a greater capacity to do so at this stage of our journey. Nonetheless, we can give ourselves permission to start feeling hope. We have new possibilities of reinventing ourselves with relationships, hobbies, and career paths that are different than we had expected. Exploring those options might once again give us glimpses of what happiness feels like.

**"MOVING FORWARD WITH GRIEF"**
Nora McInerny is a young widow whose husband died of brain cancer. In a memorable TED Talk, she notes that grief is not something we ever fully leave behind: "We don't 'move on' from grief. We move forward with it . . . What can we do other than try to remind one another that some things can't be fixed, and not all wounds are meant to heal? We need each other to remember, to help each other remember, that grief is this multitasking emotion. That you can and will be sad, and happy; you'll be grieving, and able to love in the same year or week, the same breath. We need to remember that a grieving person is going to laugh again and smile again. If they're lucky, they'll even find love again. But yes, absolutely, they're going to move forward. But that doesn't mean they've moved on."[20]

**Story 5 Suggestions:** We can help each other reach acceptance by listening, celebrating the past, encouraging each other to try new things, and setting hopeful goals for the future. This might be a time to change our physical environment to reflect our new life by donating a loved one's things to charity or remodeling the spare bedroom into a proper home office. Perhaps we'll add meditation or involvement with a faith community to our daily or weekly routine. Taking classes or developing new hobbies may bring us into contact with a new circle of friends who can bring more fulfillment to life.

In our post-pandemic schools, let's start looking to the future instead of nostalgically longing to recreate the past. What worked and what didn't about online education? How can we use technology more effectively in hybrid learning models going forward? How can we partner with parents who want to play a greater role in their children's education? Now that we understand better than ever the unhealthy outcomes of extended social isolation, how can we create a more connected community? Solutions may be surprisingly low-cost. In Great Britain, citizens concerned about the effects of social isolation began posting signs on park benches inviting lonely strangers to sit and converse. "Happy to Chat" benches have now become a worldwide phenomenon.[21]

Winston Churchill once said, "Never let a good crisis go to waste." As unwelcome and damaging as they may be, crises are imbued with opportunity. When we've reached a place of acceptance ourselves, we have the opportunity to show genuine leadership. Now is the time to cast a bold, innovative, and creative vision for the future. Now is the time to invite others who are ready to move forward to follow us into new chapters, new adventures, and yes, new storms. But we've already proven we can handle those.

> "Never let a good crisis go to waste." - Winston Churchill

**"YOU CAN'T STOP THE WAVES,
BUT YOU CAN LEARN TO RIDE THEM"**[22]

How can we learn to accept things as they are . . . while still working steadily for a brighter future?

Here are some suggestions:

1. **Understand what you can and can't control.** You are not powerless. Make a three-column chart of things you can control, things you can influence, and things you can't control. Focus your energy on the first two columns.

2. **Get comfortable with uncertainty.** While you can't solve the pandemic, racism, wildfires, or violence, understand that you can *manage* these adaptive challenges in your school community.

3. **Stop resisting reality.** Fighting the inevitable adds more stress. "If the problem can be solved, why worry? If the problem cannot be solved, worrying will do you no good." - Buddha

4. **Reframe.** Rather than, "This crisis is killing us," try "Getting through this crisis will strengthen our school community."

5. **Celebrate and appreciate others.** Taking a strengths-based approach to others helps you learn to accept things . . . and people . . . as they are.

## Trauma: Riding Out a Tsunami

How does trauma impact the grieving process? Trauma is a psychological response to a deeply threatening event, such as a car accident, illness, death, rape, or assault. Different people may experience different levels of trauma from similar events depending on their past experiences and coping skills. After the initial shock and denial, a victim may continue to experience anger, sadness, flashbacks, volatile emotions, physical symptoms, guilt, shame, and hopelessness.[23]

Trauma reactions can cause a person to get stuck in an unresolved story of grief, such as denial, anger, bargaining, or depression, and to have difficulty moving on to a healthy level of acceptance. People may even backtrack from acceptance to earlier grief reactions in response to triggering circumstances. Trauma changes the brain structure in ways that increase the individual's fear-based emotional responses to stimuli and keep them in a constant state of hypervigilance, contributing to sleep disturbances, flashbacks, and impaired memory. Over the long term, trauma can lead to early death by making the survivor more susceptible to physical disease, risk-taking, and addictive behaviors.[24]

It is not the presence of trauma itself that will determine how deeply it impacts someone's life, but how the individual responds to it.[25] Not all of our students experienced COVID-19 as a traumatic event, though many did. But even in "normal" times, our classrooms are full of traumatized students. Adverse Childhood Experiences (ACEs) are potentially traumatic events—such as abuse, neglect, substance abuse, violence, or mental illness in the household—that happen before the age of 18.[26] ACEs affect an estimated 60% of the general population, and even more of the population among those who live in high poverty or other risk areas. Young children exposed to five or more significant adverse experiences in the first three years of childhood face a 76% likelihood of having one or more delays in their language, emotional, or brain development.[27] ACEs have been linked to poor academic performance, behavioral issues, and a higher risk of chronic disease, addiction, and suicide.[28]

## A TEENAGER'S VIEW OF THE PANDEMIC

In a mass disaster event, trauma is not necessarily an experience all will have, and among those who do experience trauma, not all will process it in the same ways. Liz is a 16-year-old student in a suburban Midwestern high school. Notice the variety of reactions she and her friends had to the lockdown restrictions in the early stages of the pandemic. What interventions, if any, might each of these students need as they work through stages of grief or post-traumatic recovery?

"The pandemic didn't have much of an impact on me, really. At least not at first. None of my family or friends are high risk, so I didn't think it was a big deal. Actually, when school first shut down I was really excited. I needed a break. As the days passed I started missing my friends, but after a while it was hard staying in touch and I spent most of my time doing homework and stuff with my family. I decided to improve myself during lockdown. I wrote stories and journaled, did different kinds of art, and started exercising and doing yoga.

Some of my friends had a hard time with it. Kyle spent most of his time indoors playing video games in his room. He's kind of withdrawn anyway so he liked it. He decided to keep on doing school from home when the school reopened and they gave us the choice. But when he stayed home by himself for a long time he got super depressed and only started to get better when he got back into school in 2021. I was worried about him.

My best friend Carter had a lot of family problems before the pandemic. She liked going to school to escape from home. During the COVID thing, her family fought even more than usual and were mean to the kids. They didn't have a lot of money and had to keep their business open during the lockdown so it wouldn't go out of business. She had to work in the family business, keep up with school online, and babysit her little sister. She couldn't wait to get back to school.

I guess it did affect my friends a lot but I'm glad it wasn't bad for me. I don't want to do it again though. Everybody around me was so stressed out."

## How Common are ACES?

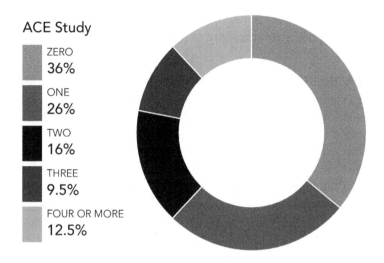

ACE Study

| | |
|---|---|
| ZERO | **36%** |
| ONE | **26%** |
| TWO | **16%** |
| THREE | **9.5%** |
| FOUR OR MORE | **12.5%** |

*"Aces and Resilience" chart adapted from SAFEchildRaleigh NC, https://safechildnc.org/aces-and-resilience/*

In an actual tsunami, the best way to survive is to get to higher ground and avoid it altogether. But for a person in a boat who can't make it to shore in time, it's best actually to face the tsunami and take your boat right into it and over it. In shallow water, tsunamis rise to greater heights and destructive power, while out in deep water, an energetic tsunami might pass right under a ship without even being felt.[29] Similarly, trauma therapy helps to deepen an individual's resources to face their fear and navigate through it skillfully. Therapists have found Cognitive Behavioral Therapy, exposure therapy, and talk therapy to be effective treatment modalities for trauma. Mindfulness meditation, yoga, neurofeedback, and EMDR (Eye Movement Desensitization and Reprocessing) have also been helpful.[30] Trauma is a serious issue that most of us are not trained to diagnose and treat properly, but we can increase our capacity to recognize it, respond to it, and build a supportive institutional culture.

### 1. RECOGNIZING TRAUMA

Warning signs of trauma can include disruptions to eating and sleeping patterns; low energy; withdrawal; unexplained aches and pains; feelings of guilt, worry, helplessness, and hopelessness; substance abuse; and suicidal ideation. Children and teens may compete more than usual for attention, be unwilling to leave home, have difficulty concentrating, or become more aggressive and disruptive.[31] Trauma-informed parents, teachers, and administrators who recognize these symptoms may understand the need to treat some disruptive student behavior not as a disciplinary issue but as a mental health crisis, and help find appropriate professional assistance as needed.

### 2. INCREASING FACULTY CAPACITY TO RESPOND TO TRAUMA

Investing faculty development dollars into mental health training is a wise, proactive step. In an actual tsunami, the first wave may not be the largest in a series of waves. Likewise, the pandemic will likely bring years of traumatic aftereffects that require proactive preparation. A nationwide survey of college faculty members from January through March 2021 found that 80% of them had dealt with student mental health issues, although only 30% had been trained to do so. 70% indicated they would welcome training in this area.[32] This certainly seems like a case in which faculty demands are congruent with the best interests of the students and the institution.

### 3. INCREASING FACULTY EFFICACY

One of the pervasive effects of trauma is a sense of powerlessness and hopelessness that can leave a person paralyzed when action needs to be taken. Efficacy, by contrast, is the belief of an individual or group that they have the ability to achieve their goals. Efficacy can be both individual and collective—both "I believe that I am able to achieve my goals" and "We as a group believe we are well-positioned to achieve our goals." How can we expand the capacity of those we lead through this kind of empowered thinking?

Many teachers have intrinsic capacity. They comprehend the rationale for a particular practice, have the knowledge to adapt it to their classrooms, and are able to evaluate its effectiveness. This capacity goes to waste if we don't know about it and if we don't complement it with extrinsic capacity, such as training and support, consistent leadership, and well-designed and equipped classroom environments.

Chad was a third grader with Oppositional Defiance Disorder (ODD) who had bounced between several area schools. His violent fits of rage had physically injured staff. As I puzzled over which of our teachers would be the best fit for him, Mrs. Arnold, one of our most introverted, soft-spoken teachers, walked into my office and announced, "I want Chad for my room. I'm the best teacher for him. I have a brother who had the same issues." The school counselor, special education director, and I came together to provide the support Mrs. Arnold needed, including regular check-ins and opportunities to attend courses and training sessions to get more ideas and strategies. Her experience with Chad wasn't easy, but as we brought together intrinsic and extrinsic capacity, he made remarkable progress.

## 4. INCREASING COLLECTIVE EFFICACY

How can we build a sense of collective efficacy in our campuses? It grows through our daily practices. We need to use a common vocabulary, making sure the campus is clear about what we mean and that it is aligned with our institutional mission. To avoid misunderstanding, norms need to be articulated rather than left unspoken. We can increase efficacy by breaking down silos within the institution—for example, by setting up projects that will require interdepartmental collaboration. Alignment and engagement must be increased. Used correctly, standardized testing and other measurements can help schools evaluate whether they are achieving best practices and standards.

Collective efficacy is greatly facilitated by the way leaders influence the narrative of the school. If the narrative is focused on test scores, compliance to procedures, and schedules, the school community will perceive these as important to learning. If the narrative focuses on learning, executive function skills, managing the thinking process, and respectful collaboration, the school community will begin to think of learning differently. Leaders need to use their influence to create a narrative that leads to a culture of belonging that values and empowers all members of the school community.

## Looking Back, Looking Ahead

We've seen that human beings have some established patterns for handling grief. Though these patterns vary with the individual, they contribute to how we adjust emotionally to loss and integrate it into our life's story so that we can continue on our journey to identity, significance, belonging, and hope. Trauma breaks down our usual processes for managing grief and we have difficulty reconciling with our loss and moving forward. Managing trauma often requires professional help, but we can increase our capacity to recognize trauma, our faculty's capacity to respond to it, and our faculty's sense of their own individual efficacy and that of the institution. The end result of all of this can be an institutional culture that is empowering and supportive to people at all stages of grief and trauma, one that can continue moving forward even while the healing process is far from over.

## REFLECTION QUESTIONS

1. How have your experiences of grief, either through the COVID-19 crisis or personal events in your life, caused you to grow? How have they impacted your appreciation of life?

2. What are some meaningful ways you can build relationships with friends and colleagues who are working through stages of grief? What do you think a real friend would do at each stage?

3. What new possibilities has the disruption of the pandemic opened up for you? What suggestion from this chapter did you find most helpful in thinking about how to explore those new opportunities?

### STRAIGHTFORWARD SURVIVAL

When we experience disruption, sometimes we need simple ideas for taking a next, practical step forward. If you are unsure of where to start, choose one of these ideas from the chapter:

- Commit to listening to others. Who can you give undistracted attention today?

- Practice validating the feelings of others.

- Build the efficacy and capacity of the school staff. What can the team take on?

## ENDNOTES

1. W. Khairy, (2014, November 22). "Film Analysis: 'The Babadook,'" *The Cinephile Fix*. Retrieved February 24, 2022, from https://cinephilefix.com/2014/11/22/film-analysis-the-babadook/ .

2. S. Sophie, (2021, December 1), "2021 Atlantic Hurricane Season was the Third Most Active on Record - and the Most Costly," *CBS News*. Retrieved February 25, 2022, from https://www.cbsnews.com/news/hurricane-season-2021-third-most-active-most-costly.

3. K. Reid, (2020, June 4), "2004 Indian Ocean Earthquake and Tsunami: Facts, FAQs, and How to Help," World Vision. Retrieved February 25, 2022, from https://www.worldvision.org/disaster-relief-news-stories/2004-indian-ocean-earthquake-tsunami-facts.

4. F. C. Schaefer, et al., (2012), *Trauma & Resilience: A Handbook: Effectively Supporting Those Who Serve God*. Condeo Press. 5-6

5. Wilson, D. (2014, May 27). *9 Trigger Warnings for Hamlet*. The Federalist. Retrieved May 2, 2022, from https://thefederalist.com/2014/05/27/9-trigger-warnings-for-hamlet/.

6. L. Phillips, (2021, May 4), "Untangling Trauma and Grief After Loss." *Counseling Today*. Retrieved February 25, 2022, from https://ct.counseling.org/2021/05/untangling-trauma-and-grief-after-loss/.

7. G. Elerick, (2022, Mar. 1), "We Grieve So We Can Connect." American Psychological Association. Retrieved March 1, 2022, from https://www.linkedin.com/pulse/we-grieve-so-can-connect-american-psychological-association/.

8. A. Liner, (n.d.), "The 5 Stages of Grief and How to Get Through Them." Retrieved February 28, 2022, from https://www.fluxpsychology.com/blog/the-5-stages-of-grief-and-how-to-get-through-them.

9. "Syrian Father Teaches Daughter to Cope With Bombs Through Laughter," (2020, February 18), AFP News Agency. Retrieved February 28, 2022, from https://www.youtube.com/watch?v=4cvH7aHfE5A.

10. "First Stage of Grief: Denial," (n.d.), eCondolence.com. Retrieved February 28, 2022, from https://www.econdolence.com/learning-center/grief-and-coping/the-stages-of-grief/first-stage-of-grief-denial.

11. "Second Stage of Grief: Anger," (n.d.), eCondolence.com. Retrieved February 28, 2022, from https://www.econdolence.com/learning-center/grief-and-coping/the-stages-of-grief/second-stage-of-grief-anger/.

12. "2021 Unruly Passenger Data," (2022, February 22), Federal Aviation Administration. Retrieved February 28, 2022, from https://www.faa.gov/data_research/passengers_cargo/unruly_passengers/2021_archive/.

13. K. Coleman, (2021, November 2), "You Could Get Banned From Flying for Do-

ing This," *Best Life*. Retrieved February 28, 2022, from https://bestlifeonline.com/banned-from-flying-news/.

14. "Second Stage of Grief: Anger," (n.d.), eCondolence.com. Retrieved February 28, 2022, from https://www.econdolence.com/learning-center/grief-and-coping/the-stages-of-grief/second-stage-of-grief-anger/.

15. "Third Stage of Grief: Bargaining," (n.d.), eCondolence.com. Retrieved February 28, 2022, from https://www.econdolence.com/learning-center/grief-and-coping/the-stages-of-grief/third-stage-of-grief-bargaining/.

16. "Therapists' Tips for Working Through the Stages of Grief," (2020, December 10), *Talkspace*. Retrieved February 28, 2022, from https://www.talkspace.com/blog/stages-of-grief-therapists-advice-grieving/.

17. "Fourth Stage of Grief: Depression," (n.d.), eCondolence.com. Retrieved March 1, 2022, from https://www.econdolence.com/learning-center/grief-and-coping/the-stages-of-grief/fourth-stage-of-grief-depression/.s

18. "Hidden Signs of Depression: How to Spot Them and What to do," *Medical News Today*. MediLexicon International. Retrieved March 1, 2022, from https://www.medicalnewstoday.com/articles/325513#forced-happiness.

19. "Fifth Stage of Grief: Acceptance," (n.d.), eCondolence.com. Retrieved March 1, 2022, from https://www.econdolence.com/learning-center/grief-and-coping/the-stages-of-grief/fifth-stage-of-grief-acceptance/.

20. McInerny, N. (n.d.). *We don't "Move on" from grief. we move forward with it.* Nora McInerny: We don't "move on" from grief. We move forward with it | TED Talk. Retrieved April 4, 2022, from https://www.ted.com/talks/nora_mcinerny_we_don_t_move_on_from_grief_we_move_forward_with_it?language=en.

21. M. Lloyd, (2019, October 18), "'Happy to Chat' Benches: The Woman Getting Strangers to Talk," BBC News. Retrieved March 1, 2022, from https://www.bbc.com/news/uk-wales-50000204.

22. "Get inspired!" (2021, September 15), *The Main Idea*. Retrieved February 17, 2022, from https://www.themainidea.net/get-inspired/.

23. Rosen, A. et al. (2021, August 23). *"What is trauma?"* The Center for Treatment of Anxiety and Mood Disorders. Retrieved March 1, 2022, from https://centerforanxietydisorders.com/what-is-trauma/.

24. Dass-Brailsford, P. (2007). *A Practical approach to trauma: Empowering interventions*. SAGE Publications. 32-34.

25. G. Vaccaro, J. Lavick, J., (2008, July 1), "Trauma: Frozen Moments, Frozen Lives." *TheBody*. Retrieved March 1, 2022, from https://www.thebody.com/content/art48754.html.

26. "Adverse Childhood Experiences," (n.d.), National Conference of State Legislatures. Retrieved March 1, 2022, from https://www.ncsl.org/research/health/adverse-childhood-experiences-aces.aspx.

27. "Adverse Childhood Experiences (ACES)," (2019, November 5), Centers for Disease Control and Prevention. Retrieved February 10, 2022, from https://www.cdc.gov/vitalsigns/aces/index.html.

28. Ibid.

29. J. Piven, (2001), *The Worst-Case Scenario Survival Handbook Travel.* Findaway World. 136-7.

30. A. Rosen, et al., (2021, August 23), "What Is Trauma?" The Center for Treatment of Anxiety and Mood Disorders. Retrieved March 1, 2022, from https://centerforanxietydisorders.com/what-is-trauma/.

31. "Warning Signs and Risk Factors for Emotional Distress," (n.d.), SAMHSA. Retrieved March 1, 2022, from https://www.samhsa.gov/find-help/disaster-distress-helpline/warning-signs-risk-factors.

32. J. Piven, (2001), *The Worst-Case Scenario Survival Handbook Travel.* Findaway World. 136-7.

33. J. McKoy, (2021, April 15), "Majority of US Faculty Members Help Students Deal with Mental Health Issues--But Few are Trained to Do So," *The Brink,* Boston University. Retrieved March 1, 2022, from https://www.bu.edu/articles/2021/majority-of-us-faculty-members-help-students-deal-with-mental-health-issues-but-few-are-trained-to-do-so/.

# CHAPTER 3: RESTORING FOCUS
## Keeping the Boat Upright and on Course

James and Naomi pulled up in front of the school in an Omaha suburb, ready to pick up their kids from band practice. There were severe thunderstorm warnings that afternoon, so they arrived early and were parked close to the entrance. Soon a steady drumbeat of large raindrops made conversation impossible. Hailstones the size of quarters began pelting their car and the sky took on a greenish cast. By the time the tornado sirens sounded, gale force winds were blowing the rain horizontally and their car began rocking back and forth. Envisioning the car potentially being thrown across the parking lot by a tornado, James panicked, threw open the driver's side door, and dashed toward the school, while Naomi gathered her purse and took her husband's abandoned keys from the ignition before joining his flight. As they ran across the lawn to the front door of the school, a powerful gust suddenly blew them both headlong into the ground. Stunned and bedraggled, they struggled back to their feet and ran into the school, minus their glasses, keys, and half the contents of Naomi's purse. With classic Midwestern stoicism, the school custodian, who had been watching from inside, held the door open for them and commented, "Wind's pickin' up, ain't it?"

Fortunately Naomi and James weren't physically injured, though as they later learned, a small tornado actually did touch down not far away, doing minor damage to fences, trees, and the siding of a few dozen homes. The couple's alarm had been legitimate, and quickly getting into the school was a good decision. However, faced with the same crisis, James panicked while Naomi took a more focused, methodical approach. In the end, they both got through the storm with recoverable losses, but Naomi felt far less traumatized by it—and saw more humor in it—than James, who felt he'd had a near-death experience and even had nightmares about it afterward.

Our individual personalities, coping skills, and previous life experiences inform each of our approaches to unexpected traumas. Some people have a stronger ability to stay focused under pressure; others get thrown off by relatively small distractions. These tendencies can be so deeply ingrained that completely changing them is unreasonable, but everyone can expand their repertoire of tools to stay focused in tense and chaotic circumstances. It's essential that we increase our ability to focus on the critical tasks at hand without losing sight of the strategic steps we must continue to take toward our desired future. In another manner of speaking, in a storm, not only do we need to keep our boat upright, we need to keep it on course.

> In a storm, not only do we need to keep our boat upright, we need to keep it on course.

## Why Do We Lose Focus?

Rashid, a school district leader, told me during the pandemic, "At this point, it's about figuring out what is most important to the most people to keep us open and somewhat engaged. Everyone is at capacity." This quote could have easily come from any one of thousands of leaders across the country, struggling just to do the basics: stay open and at least somewhat engaged. But it may be hard to stay focused even on those basic goals when our brains are trying to process the demanding stimuli of a major crisis. Some reasons we get off target are related to the inherent survival mechanisms of our brains, while others are the result of our environments and cultural conditioning that fill our lives with harmful distractions in even the best of times.

### FIGHT, FLIGHT, FREEZE, OR FAWN

Timothy Strauman, professor of psychology and neuroscience at Duke University, says that "disrupted focus and lower energy are your brain's response to the pandemic."[1] When faced with a life-threatening situation, our brains are wired to ignore everything except the immediate threat.

"COVID-19 is this once-in-a-lifetime event that disrupts our focus and puts our desires on hold [while] we're more focused on surviving."[2]

The so-called "fight or flight" stress response is a protective mechanism that goes into motion automatically when we feel threatened. To these two classic options, some psychologists add the options of "freeze" and "fawn." Thus, perceiving a threat, our body responds with one of four typical reactions:

- **Fight:** aggressively confronting the perceived threat.
- **Flight:** running away from the danger.
- **Freeze:** becoming unable to move or act against a threat.
- **Fawn:** trying to please and deflect to avoid conflict.

These responses can be triggered not only by an actual life-threatening situation, but by the perception of danger, which in a previously traumatized person can occur as a result of seemingly innocuous triggers. When this happens, the amygdala signals the hypothalamus to stimulate the autonomic nervous system. The body responds by releasing the stress hormones adrenaline and cortisol, which speed up the heart rate and respiration to take more oxygen to major muscle groups, leaving our hands and feet feeling cold. Sight and hearing become sharper as we try to assess danger. Our body even prepares for possible injury by reducing our ability to perceive pain and by thickening the blood to enhance its clotting properties. With all these extreme physiological changes taking place, there is a decrease in activity in the prefrontal cortex of the brain where higher thinking and rational decision-making take place. It becomes difficult to string thoughts together logically as our minds and bodies are overwhelmed with the task of detecting and overcoming threats, real or imagined.[3] After the feeling of threat has passed, it usually takes 20-30 minutes to return to our natural state...assuming no other perceived threats have arisen in that time.[4]

## MEMORY CONSOLIDATION

During traumatic circumstances, not only are our brains processing overwhelming danger signals and the turbulent emotional flood they bring, we also are trying to store new experiences in our memories in ways that make sense to us. Consolidation theory hypothesizes how the brain consolidates new memories and adds them to old memories, connecting the new memories to previous experience and strengthening our ability to recall them. System consolidation theory suggests that the hippocampus consolidates new memories before storing them in other locations in the brain. Reconsolidation theory posits that old memories are reactivated and then supplemented and modified.[5] Either way, during a traumatic event, not only is our brain running on survival mode, it's attempting to make sense of what is happening and encode new memories together with the most relevant categories of old memories. A tall order, and one that is likely to result in the faulty recall of information, as well as confusion and misinterpretation.

## MULTITASKING

Multitasking is a major disruptor of deep focus. In one survey, 97% of participants said that multitasking made them more efficient,[6] when in fact researchers say that "decades of research indicate the quality of one's output and depth of thought deteriorate as one attends to ever more tasks."[7] John Grafman, chief of Cognitive Neuroscience at the National Institute of Neurological Disorders and Stroke, says that during multitasking, individuals typically do not complete activities in as much depth and become content with superficial performance.[8] If multitasking is such a disruptor of our deep focus in regular life, it's no great leap of imagination to understand how much more disruptive it becomes with the additional tasks and unfamiliar routines of a fast-moving crisis.

## INTERRUPTIONS

Interruptions are another common source of disruption that multiplies in times of crisis, especially for those in leadership positions. Research shows it takes a person 23 minutes to refocus at work after a disruption.[9] In a crisis, an entire day can easily be consumed with an endless stream of interruptions, leaving us feeling that we have made no progress toward our own most important priorities because we've been taking care of other people's issues.

## TRIVIAL PURSUITS

In crisis, with our minds experiencing an existential "brainstorm" on top of all the typical disruptions that are now dramatically intensified by the circumstances, what do we do?

I don't know about you, but I clean out my email. I delete old emails, respond to things from last year that don't really matter anymore. I put things I might want to see later in neat, organized folders. Science fiction writer Robert A. Heinlein wrote, "In the absence of clearly defined goals, we become strangely loyal to performing daily trivia until ultimately we become enslaved by it."[10] In my experience, even with clearly defined goals, it is human nature to substitute easily manageable tasks for those that we dread because of their complexity or ambiguity. We end up becoming people who are busy, but not productive.

## IS BURNOUT A CHOICE?[11]

Rachel Druckenmiller was only 32 years old when she went to her doctor with a sore throat, swollen lymph nodes, fatigue, a cough, and congestion, feeling worse than she'd ever felt in her life. It wasn't COVID-19: It was the physical manifestation of burnout caused by a life driven by career. Rachel came to see this burnout as a self-inflicted wound. She was intensely driven to succeed, to prove herself in response to her deep-seated assumption that "Who I am is not enough." To beat burnout, Rachel says we must do some painful self-reflection. Consider:

1. What assumptions are we making about what will happen if we slow down, ask for help, or say no?

2. How much of our burnout results from our assumptions, expectations, or pride?

3. What is the need beneath our striving and achieving, and can it be met through something other than working harder?

4. Have we built healthy practices of journaling, therapy, coaching, or spiritual support?

5. How many things have we said yes to out of guilt or obligation? Can any of those be dropped, delayed, or delegated to create more margin for ourselves?

   Wayne Muller said, "If we do not allow for a rhythm of rest in our overly-busy lives, illness becomes our sabbath."[12] The question is not whether we will rest. Our bodies will take what they need to survive, even if that means landing us in the hospital. The question is, will we plan our rest wisely to create a life balance that is continually renewing our ability to be productive—and enjoy life?

## How Can Individuals Regain Focus?

Individuals seeking to regain disrupted focus must first learn to recognize the "fight, flight, freeze, or fawn" reaction and begin to manage it. Although rational thought becomes more difficult in this aroused state, if we can retain the presence of mind to realize it is happening, we might shift our focus to soothing ourselves, rather than engaging in a conflict or giving way to panic. Three types of approaches can be helpful to us, both to prepare ourselves for distressing situations and to step back from the ledge when we find ourselves in them:

1. **Relaxation techniques:** take a deep breath, visualize yourself in a calmer situation, meditate mindfully, pray, or use any other technique to slow your breathing and heart rate to normal.

2. **Physical activity:** take a walk, do a few push-ups, or do some vigorous house cleaning. Exercise decreases stress hormones, increases endorphins, and promotes calm.

3. **Social support:** talk to someone who helps you feel safe. Getting a calmer, more objective perspective on what's bothering you, or just being in the presence of someone you trust and who is not agitated, can help you feel calmer.[13]

Once we get past overwhelming feelings of fear or anger that disrupt our focus, how do we get ourselves together to start moving in a focused way and resume accomplishing important tasks? Most people have their own favorite productivity methods; if you don't, you can find ideas by the hundreds online. What works will be specific to the individual. The following brief narrative will highlight for us some useful tips:

Sofia, a clinical psychologist, had to transition to working from home at the start of the pandemic in March 2020. In the midst of all she had to do in the upheaval, tension, fear, and uncertainty of those early days of the pandemic . . . she decided to paint her daughter's room. She went to the building supply store, selected a sample color, painted a square of gray paint on the wall to see how it looked, then promptly lost all motivation and did nothing more about it. As the months passed, she grew tired of being reminded of yet another unfinished task, so she simply taped one of her daughter's drawings over the accusing paint dab. "I had these ambitious goals for me and my kids when we started being at home full-time," she explained. "I needed to reprioritize. Painting the room wasn't a necessity. I needed to figure out how to work from home. I needed to figure out how to get settled." But Sofia didn't just work on higher priority tasks. She also rested. Until the pandemic, she had always stayed busy with housework, errands, and office work she had brought home. In fact, painting the room was just another way of keeping herself as busy as she had always been. But a few months into the pandemic, she started taking the occasional 30-minute power nap. The results? "It was the best thing ever. I never would have allowed myself to do that before the pandemic. I felt so restored."[14]

Sofia's story is all too familiar to most of us. It brings up several themes we should consider:

- Lack of focus can and does affect us all. Sofia is a professional, in psychology no less, yet disrupted focus could throw her off track as easily as anyone else.

- Unfinished projects don't have to be a source of shame. Sometimes they're even characteristic of a creative, curious, and high-capacity person.

- An appropriate response to a crisis is to prioritize the most important things, which may be about psychological and relational health as much as physical survival.

- Strategic times of rest are not only advisable, they are essential. Not only do we need enough sleep, we need regular breaks during the day to stay at our peak mental and physical performance. After all, am I working to live, or living to work?

> Am I working to live,
> or living to work?

## How Can Institutions Regain Focus?

To keep educational institutions focused, we need clarity about our desired outcomes. Assessments of various sorts are essential to tracking progress toward certain academic goals, but "teaching to the test" can be disruptive to a school's broader mission and vision. Desired outcomes are affected by the climate and culture of a campus. For our discussion, climate and culture are not synonymous. Dr. Justin Tarte offers this humorous explanation: "School climate is what is said in a staff faculty meeting. School culture is what is said in the parking lot after the meeting."[15] Understanding a school's climate and culture can guide us in setting campus priorities, reframing the story of the school, and reimagining the future.

One priority on all campuses is safety. Ever-present worries about school shootings faded somewhat during the pandemic as safety concerns shifted to virus protection issues: mask mandates, social distancing, sanitizing, quarantining, contact tracing. Alienation and divisiveness over these issues have pushed many to the boiling point. As we have returned to our brick-and-mortar buildings, many education professionals are becoming more aware of the increased mental health crisis we have been thrown into as we continue to process the fallout of the disruptions of the past two years. Physical safety is critical, but true safety is deeper than that. True safety encompasses social, emotional, intellectual, and physical safety, which set a foundation to help students learn and develope important developmental and future-ready skills. We can spend hours in heated discussions over ways to try to build a bigger fence to keep trouble out of our campuses, but schools must address safety from the inside out. School safety and wellness are critically important for our school communities, but there are many people in those communities who may not understand how safety is enhanced by understanding trauma, developing social skills, and creating a culture of compassion. This is one area where the leadership must lead.

## DEATH BY 1,000 PAPER CUTS

"I'm not sure I can keep these training dates for our leadership. We have been back and forth between online, hybrid, and face-to-face all this past semester. Our leaders are in the most dismal mood I've ever seen them." Kate was assistant superintendent in a district that had engaged me for leadership training before the shutdown. I was trying to develop an aligned set of student-centric learning experiences to prepare students authentically for the future. "Oh Kate, I'm so sorry. Is there anything I can do to help?" I asked. In resignation, Kate replied, "I don't know. We've lost our focus but I don't know what to do about it. We are at our wits' end just dealing with the day-to-day. It's like death by 1,000 paper cuts."

Kate's district was beset with challenges. The once-thriving surrounding community had been hit hard over the past two decades by the withdrawal of major manufacturers and the resulting loss of jobs. The effects of trauma were visible throughout the schools and community. Poverty, violence, and other effects of urban decay overflowed into the schools. The district's tax base and school funding were declining. Their graduation rate and test scores were extremely low. Many of the leaders didn't even live in the district. The mentality was one of survival; there was a general feeling of "everyone for themselves."

Kate and the district's relatively new superintendent had spent a couple of years toiling to build cohesiveness between their people and programs. They had implemented a plan to help focus their energies on programs, processes, and priorities that engaged students and helped them see a successful path forward. Then COVID hit. With limited resources, Kate and her colleagues tried to brainstorm an equitable way to get their few available computers into the hands of students. They couldn't find many good options. Their technology budget had already been drained in equipping classrooms with what they needed; there was little overflow for an emergency switch to virtual classrooms. When lockdown was announced one day in March 2020, many of the district's students went home never to return. For those who did not drop out, learning was so severely disrupted that the rest of the year was a wash.

The COVID relief funds provided to schools by the federal government were especially welcome in Kate's district, but brought on additional responsibilities. District personnel had to strategize and plan how best to use the new funds to provide the most impact for students. These planning meetings were exciting at first. The new funding meant new possibilities for providing resources and programming for students, the chance to help them catch up and prepare for a strong return in the fall. But before long came a sense of disappointment . It was a violent summer in the community. Crime increased, several schools were burglarized, and there was a stabbing right outside one of the middle schools. Gang-related activity created a never-ending cycle of violence and retaliation. The administrators and teachers were intensely committed to their students. They wanted to help, but there were only so many hours in the day, and only so many crises their psyches could handle simultaneously.

Remember the student-centric vision Kate and the new superintendent were trying to implement before COVID? The one they had spent a full two years carefully planning and weaving relationships to implement? Out of necessity, when COVID hit, the administration immediately shifted their focus from their desired future to a RIGHT NOW orientation. Teachers had to go back to methods taken from an earlier era, methods that did not live up to the administration's high hopes for learner-centered education. For Kate, it was demoralizing to invest years in plans to make a real difference, only to find that the she could do was keep alive a badly wounded system that was far from ideal in the first place.

There's a difference between leading to survive and leading to thrive. Thriving requires us to look ahead and make bold decisions. Surviving is more about managing immediate needs that arise. Surviving is not what most leaders signed up for. The teacher shortage has been well documented. Less well known is what's happening with school leaders. Even before the pandemic, principals weren't lasting long in their jobs. A 2009 study of more than 16,900 principals in Texas showed their average tenure on the job was only 3.38-4.96 years.[16] "There's no doubt that we are seeing the greatest exodus of leadership at the district level that we have seen in this country," Dan Domenech, Executive Director of the School Superintendents Association (AASA), told *Newsweek*.[17] In 2021, about 25% of superintendents nationwide left their jobs, a sharp escalation from previous years. Some of the main reasons cited included the COVID-19 pandemic, staff shortages, disagreements over Critical Race Theory, and rancorous school board meetings[18]—in other words, a set of disruptions that have distracted leaders and their districts from staying on course to a bold and better future.

> There's a difference between leading to survive and leading to thrive. Thriving requires us to look ahead and make bold decisions. Surviving is more about managing immediate needs that come up.

"Death by a thousand paper cuts" is an apt description of the struggle of school leaders. Our focus is disrupted by too many demands with too limited a workforce to handle them, even in the best of times. In a crisis, maintaining focus seems impossible. But giving up is not an option. To use the analogy of a wartime situation, we have to do the tough triage necessary to win the fight for our children and their future. Paper cuts are painful, but every one of them does not require immediate attention. We must stop the heavy bleeding first, then prioritize how to handle the rest.

Perhaps we'll even find that if our priorities are right, some of those cuts will even heal on their own.

## DELEGATION

An African proverb goes like this: "If you want to go fast, go alone. If you want to go far, go together." We live in a world of instant gratification and immediate criticism. We feel internal and external pressure to fix every minor problem now. Constantly attending to tedious tasks takes leaders' attention away from the long-range focus that they are uniquely qualified to provide. Even as we weather a crisis, it's important to develop leaders within your district and campus. We can start by considering who is currently part of our leadership team. What are their strengths? Are there any gaps that our current team is not able to cover?

> "If you want to go fast, go alone. If you want to go far, go together." - African proverb

Like many of us, my friend Dave, a school leader, struggled with delegation. He didn't want to put anything else on his overburdened teachers. Laura, his administrative assistant, had been out with COVID and now her children had it. Now many of Dave's important administrative tasks had fallen two weeks behind. He was doing as much as he could and looked haggard.

"What are your options?" I asked him. "We can't make the day longer, so what has to be done today?" Dave identified ten things of weighty importance. We were able to push two of them to a later date. Of the remainder, six could be delegated, and only two legitimately could only be done by him. Although it looked like the problem was solved, Dave continued to feel discouraged. He still saw a list of eight things he felt he had to do, because he still didn't want to burden others, and he felt it would take longer to explain how to execute them than to do them himself. Moreover, while all the tasks were important, not a single one had to do with his future vision of the school. To top it off, Dave mentioned that he would be driving a school bus the next day, due to short staffing. Dave needed help, but to receive it he needed to let go of some control—no longer deciding for himself what other people's limitations were; no longer making sure each task was done as perfectly as his assistant would have done it; no longer prioritizing getting things done fast rather than taking a little time to train other leaders to make the workflow more sustainable in the future. For a strategically vital leader, pushing to the brink of burnout with unrelated tasks like bus driving was not a wise deployment of resources.

# WHAT GETS DONE?

How do we make sure we actually accomplish the things that need to happen, especially when the proper execution of plans depends on multiple people? Drawing from business practices that apply to an educational environment, professionals at Meteor Education created the Seven Laws of What Gets Done. Which of these is practical for you to implement? How and when will you get started?

 1. **What gets pictured gets done.** Build some white space into your calendar to brainstorm, think, and innovate. You can do this alone or with your leadership team. Can you see it? Then you can bring it to life.

 2. **What gets modeled gets done.** This principle is true both in instructional practices and in daily behaviors. Are you modeling the behaviors you want see? Is your leadership team?

 3. **What gets praised gets done.** Feedback is crucial. Praise the behaviors and practices that move you further in your mission.

 4. **What gets trained gets done.** Training should be regular, tailored, and authentic to your message. It should instill a common language and a common understanding to impact your campus.

 5. **What gets measured gets done.** Without measurement, you cannot assess whether you've grown. Evidence of growth motivates us to keep going and reveals where our plans are on target.

 6. **What gets financed gets done.** Most of our plans need some kind of financing. Financing expands the number of priorities we can pursue simultaneously. When government funding is limited, how can we think outside the box to mobilize local businesses and the community to sponsor important initiatives?

 7. **What gets scheduled gets done.** Time is crucial. Great ideas generated in our brainstorming may never happen, simply because we didn't schedule them. We have to build time intentionally into our calendars for what matters, or it is unlikely to get done.

## SURVIVING THE STORM

## WHAT SHOULD WE FOCUS ON?

Leaders lead. There are many administrative and management duties in your role as a school leader, but managing and leading are different. John Kotter argues that "Management is about coping with complexity . . . Leadership, by contrast, is about coping with change." He goes on to say, "No one yet has figured out how to manage people effectively into battle; they must be led."[19] Disrupted focus can affect the ability of leaders to prioritize tasks and duties. According to the Wallace Foundation, the five key roles of school leaders are:

- Shaping a vision of academic success for all students.
- Creating a climate hospitable to education.
- Cultivating leadership in others.
- Improving instruction.
- Supporting people, data, and processes to foster school improvement. [20]

> "Management is about coping with complexity . . . Leadership, by contrast, is about coping with change." - John Kotter

## THE POWER OF A PLAN

The pandemic has provided the unique opportunity to reimagine the future of education. Disrupted focus can keep us busy with mundane tasks instead of moving toward our vision. Now is the perfect time to revisit our vision and mission. Do they still meet our needs? The power of a plan is that it moves us toward our vision, provides alignment to our mission, and can deliver focused outcomes. Leading through any change is hard, but comes with significant opportunities for growth.

There will always be many things competing for our attention. If we try to attend to too many at a time, it can contribute to burnout, inconsistency, and inadequate feedback. We can streamline how we respond to competing tasks through practical strategies. Consider making a list and then prioritizing the top 10. We can seek opinions and responses electronically when we want group input. For any given problem, we should limit ourselves to no more than three proposed solutions to ensure fidelity. And when a plan is determined, it's critical to communicate it clearly. That clear communication increases focus and alignment of both the team members and the larger school community. Here are some things to consider in making a plan that moves you and your team toward your desired future:

- **Build a "Dream Team,"** using strengths assessments to ensure that it is well-balanced. The team should be small enough to permit full participation. Larger teams should be broken down into groups of three or four for easier communication. Roles, responsibilities, and norms for the group should be explicitly clear. Key stakeholders outside of staff members such as students, business owners, or recent alumni may be included in some teams to generate fresh ideas.

- **Dream your vision.** Teams may struggle at first. Praise a lot, push a little. Team members may go only so far, and might need additional motivation to continue exploring. Define the problem, brainstorm solutions, and make sure everything is aligned to your mission statement.

- **Picture your dream.** We can't create a perfect world, but we can build a more perfect one in our minds. To prevent getting bogged down in the mundane details of the present, the whole team can begin sharing an imaginative picture of what the future could be like. Then, start working through how to bring it to life, step-by-step.

- **Share it.** The team should be able to articulate the vision. This requires some finesse, as teams need to present a consistent picture of the ultimate goal to the outside world. Every group has naysayers who are better at thinking of reasons why things can't work than ways they can. We have to remember that our goal in sharing is not to win approval, but to start casting a future-oriented vision that will become infectious, a lasting part of the school's climate and culture.

- **Allow feedback.** Those who haven't attended all the discussions may need some time to get caught up to where the group has moved. Their feedback, positive or negative, helps us understand where we're succeeding in our dream casting and where we need more work. For this process, I like to use a Google form with questions such as:

After hearing about our dreams and plans for the future, what is something you loved about what you heard?

- What do you think will be important to always keep sight of for the future?

- Is there anything you could "dream bigger" about that we haven't thought of yet?

- **Write it down.** Now is the time to articulate and wordsmith the vision. It should be worded in a way that it is accessible to and understood by all members of the school community. This vision must be communicated clearly and consistently, and followed up with action.

- **Bring it to life through a plan.** After getting the big picture in focus, specific and detailed planning can begin. The plan should be broken up into manageable chunks and laid out on a timeline. Additional stakeholders will likely need to be added to the conversation at this point.

Susan Fowler writes, "You can boost your motivation when you know you are responsible for your behavior, feel a sense of belonging, and know you have the ability to get the job done." She continues, "Notice that when you create choice, connection, and competence, you feel a sense of well-being, are in a flow state, or experience deep-seated peace."[21] A thoughtful, competent planning process can help us and our staff cut through the disruptions and focus on what moves us forward.

## A Bridge to Nowhere?

The new Choluteca Bridge in Honduras was completed in 1998 and had the distinction of being the largest bridge constructed by a Japanese company in Latin America.[22] Due to the powerful hurricanes that batter the region, state-of-the-art engineering and materials were used to make sure it could withstand the harshest weather. The very year the bridge opened, its workmanship was tested by the extraordinarily violent Hurricane Mitch, which did over $6 billion in damage to Central American infrastructure. The bridge survived the storm in pristine condition—but the Choluteca River did not fare as well. Due to the torrential rains and flooding, the river carved itself a new channel several hundred feet wide that no longer flowed under the bridge. With the roads washed out on both sides of the bridge, not only was the bridge inaccessible, it now pointlessly spanned a stretch of dry ground next to the river. Locals and the media promptly dubbed it "The Bridge to Nowhere."[23]

We've found solutions to many of the problems of our past, in our educational system, in society as a whole, and in our personal and professional lives as individuals. We have become quite adept at solving those problems. We can teach others how to solve them. But things change. Rivers alter their course and render obsolete bridges that were constructed to last a century. If we lose focus, we could find ourselves desperately trying to shore up and rebuild methods, programs, and infrastructure that have become irrelevant, instead of deploying our ingenuity and resourcefulness to bridging the new river, solving the new problems—looking at where things are now, not where they were a year ago.

Amidst an intense period of change, many things remain the same. The underlying needs in education haven't changed, any more than the need to cross the Choluteca River has. How we do it has to change, but the need is the same. What do we want from our school districts? For years educators have talked about the importance of preparing children with the skills they will need in the 21st century, and we always come back to the same themes:

- **Social skills:** collaboration and leadership
- **Emotional skills:** building resilience and self-awareness
- **Intellectual skills:** critical problem solving and innovation
- **Physical skills:** general well-being and nutrition
- **Bottom line:** we want our schools to be trustworthy stewards of our children's minds, bodies, and hearts. This is what we wanted long before the pandemic, and what we'll continue to prioritize in the years ahead.

And yet, schools can and must change. There will be growing pains. Things will look different than we remembered them, and the future will be different in some ways than we envisioned. We will grieve for things that were special to us that will not be part of our children's world. But our children may simply not need the same type of schools we've always expected them to. We will find the best way to provide them with the skills they need for the world as it is, not the world as it was or as we wish it to be. We'll use what we can of the old bridge, apply our ingenuity, and build an even better one. Some businesses boast that their products are "built to last," and that is a selling point for a house or a truck. In quickly changing fields such as technology and education, though, let's let our mantra be "built to adapt."[24]

## SURVIVING THE STORM

## REFLECTION QUESTIONS

1. When you are triggered, what tends to be your default reaction: fight, flight, freeze, or fawn? How effectively has this reaction protected you? How has it hindered you from reaching your goals?

2. What methods of regaining focus discussed in this chapter might be transferable to your students? What might be effective ways of modeling those behaviors?

3. Would you say that delegation is a strength of yours, or do you prefer to retain control of most things yourself? What are some areas in which you would be more effective if your time were freed up by delegating more responsibilities to others?

4. Did you find anything new in this chapter that can enhance your planning process? If not, were any of the suggestions something that should receive greater attention in your process?

### STRAIGHTFORWARD SURVIVAL

When we experience disruption, sometimes we need simple ideas for taking a next, practical step forward. If you are unsure of where to start, choose one of these ideas from the chapter:

- Add daily movement or exercise to your schedule.

- Sleep for eight hours each night to restore your health.

- Prioritize goals and tasks each day and delegate effectively. What can you take off your plate?

## ENDNOTES

1.  J. Black, (2020, June 22), "Disrupted Focus and Lower Energy are the Brain's Response to the Pandemic," Duke University, Department of Psychology & Neuroscience. Retrieved March 23, 2022, from https://psychandneuro.duke.edu/news/disrupted-focus-and-lower-energy-are-brain%E2%80%99s-response-pandemic.

2.  Ibid.

3.  S. Manes, (2021, January 20), "Making Sure Emotional Flooding Doesn't Capsize Your Relationship, The Gottman Institute. Retrieved March 25, 2022, from https://www.gottman.com/blog/making-sure-emotional-flooding-doesnt-capsize-your-relationship/.

4.  K. Nunez, (2020, February 21), "Fight, Flight, or Freeze: How We Respond to Threats," Healthline. Retrieved March 25, 2022, from https://www.healthline.com/health/mental-health/fight-flight-freeze#in-the-body.

5.  Kruger, (2018, July 13), "The Role of Consolidation Theory in Learning," Psychology of Education. Retrieved March 25, 2022, from https://psy3850c.wordpress.com/2018/07/13/the-role-of-consolidation-theory-in-learning.

6.  A. Deitchman, (2022), "Wait, What? On Social Network Use and Attention," Applied Psychology OPUS. Retrieved March 24, 2022, from https://wp.nyu.edu/steinhardt-appsych_opus/wait-what-on-social-network-use-and-attention/.

7.  J. D. Wallis, (2007), "Orbitofrontal Cortex and Its Contribution to Decision Making," *Annual Review of Neuroscience*, 30, 31-56. Retrieved March 24, 2022 from: https://doi.org/10.1146/annurev.neuro.30.051606.094334.

8.  Ibid.

9.  The Wallace Foundation. (2013). *The School Principal as Leader: Guiding Schools to Better Teaching and Learning.*

10. Heinlein, R. (n.d.). *Robert A. Heinlein Quotes.* Inspirational Stories. Retrieved May 2, 2022, from https://www.inspirationalstories.com/quotes/robert-a-heinlein-in-the-absence-of-clearly-defined-goals-we/.

11. R. Druckenmiller, (2022, March 10), "What's Beneath Burnout: Finding Meaning in the Mess." Retrieved April 4, 2022, from https://www.linkedin.com/pulse/whats-beneath-burnout-finding-meaning-mess-rachel-druckenmiller.

12. Muller, W. (2000). *Sabbath: Finding Rest, Renewal, and Delight in Our Busy Lives* (1st ed.). Random House Publishing Group.

13. K. Nunez, (2020, February 21), "Fight, Flight, or Freeze: How We Respond to Threats," *Healthline*. Retrieved March 25, 2022, from https://www.healthline.com/health/mental-health/fight-flight-freeze#in-the-body.

14. J. Black, (2020, June 22), "Disrupted Focus and Lower Energy are the Brain's Response to the Pandemic," Duke University, Department of Psychology & Neuroscience. Retrieved March 23, 2022, from https://psychandneuro.duke.edu/news/disrupted-focus-and-lower-energy-are-brain's-response-pandemic.

15. S. Gruenert, (2008), "School Culture, School Climate: They Are Not the Same Thing," *Principal*, 56–59.

16. The Wallace Foundation. (2013). *The School Principal as Leader: Guiding Schools to Better Reaching and Learning.*

17. J. Allen, (2022, January 15), "*Superintendent Struggle: Covid-19 Pandemic, Incivility Likely to Blame for Exodus of School Leaders, Experts Say.*" *Spokesman.* Retrieved March 23, 2022, from https://www.spokesman.com/stories/2022/jan/16/superintendent-struggle-covid-19-pandemic-incivili/.

18. S. Gruenert, (2008), "School Culture, School Climate: They Are Not the Same Thing," *Principal*, 56–59.

19. J. P. Kotter, (n.d.), "What Leaders Really Do," *Harvard Business Review.* Retrieved March 25, 2022, from https://pubmed.ncbi.nlm.nih.gov/10104518/.

20. The Wallace Foundation. (2013). *The School Principal as Leader: Guiding Schools to Better Teaching and Learning.*

21. S. Fowler, (2019), *Master Your Motivation: Three Scientific Truths for Achieving Your Goals.* Berrett-Koehler Publishers.

22. A. Juneja, (n.d.), "A Lesson From the Choluteca Bridge During COVID-19." Digital Healthcare Patient Engagement Platform. Retrieved March 24, 2022, from https://www.patientbond.com/blog/a-lesson-from-the-choluteca-bridge-during-covid-19.

23. A. Juneja, (n.d.), "A Lesson From the Choluteca Bridge During COVID-19." Digital Healthcare Patient Engagement Platform. Retrieved March 24, 2022, from https://www.patientbond.com/blog/a-lesson-from-the-choluteca-bridge-during-covid-19.

24. Ibid.

# CHAPTER 4: RESTORING RESILIENCE
## Bouncing Back Without Snapping

The school was in a high-crime neighborhood, literally caught in the crossfire of gang wars. Dinetta has grown up in the neighborhood and attended the school. She also had many adverse childhood experiences. But she bucked the odds. Supported by her grandmother, aunts, and church, she won academic and athletic scholarships, completed college, and came back to work at her old school with a drive to make a difference in her community. She was a dynamo, thinking outside the box and working tirelessly to create transformational change. The person who'd previously held her job had been an authoritarian leader. In response, Dinetta made a concerted effort to work with her teachers to build a culture of compassion. She was forthright about the challenges they faced and communicated with her school community through brutally honest optimism. She engaged proactively with the community and parents, and they knew she cared about them and the children. Through her vision-casting and determination, Dinetta had constructed a support system that accelerated students toward achieving their academic goals. Astonishingly, over the course of just two years, the school rose from an "F" rating to a "C."

All that faded to the background one morning when the school went on lockdown because of a shooting in the neighborhood. One of the students had shot and killed a former student. Another student was caught in the crossfire as she walked her brother home, and the prognosis did not look good. The police had been called to the school earlier that week due to a domestic violence issue. A teacher submitted her resignation, fearing driving through the neighborhood to school each day. "We are doing good work here," Dinetta confided in me, "but I don't know if I have it in me anymore." She was weary. Her resilience was gone, disrupted to depletion.

### 5 SUBTLE SIGNS YOU'RE HEADED FOR BURNOUT[1]

During the pandemic, 50-70% of survey respondents reported indicators of burnout. Some signs are obvious—tiredness, insomnia, irritability—but others are more subtle. Noticing these early can help us take proactive steps to change course when we're on the road to burnout. Psychologists recommend watching out for the following:

- Negative expectations: a loss of confidence, a drop in productivity, increased feelings of "imposter syndrome," a tendency to focus on easier tasks due to self-doubt, cynicism, withdrawal, and an attitude of victimization.

- Feeling underappreciated: a general sense of being overworked, underappreciated, and treated unfairly by an employer or others.

- Detaching from work: a loss of drive to excel in your career, a disinterest in workplace decisions, difficulty concentrating, procrastination, and lowered quality of work.

- Impulsive behavior: family, work, faith, and other stabilizing factors exercise less influence over you than usual, and you may begin to engage in uncharacteristic or risky behaviors, ranging from radical changes of dress or hairstyle to reckless driving or high-risk sports such as mountain climbing or skydiving.

- Becoming impatient: feeling overworked and at the end of your reserves, you become less tolerant of others and less interested in engaging in complex work.

Unaddressed burnout can be contagious to other employees. Some ways to nip it in the bud in a work environment include encouraging self-reflection in employees, helping them find ways of doing small acts of kindness toward others, and changing workplace norms to make it socially acceptable to talk about exhaustion as a problem in need of a solution—rather than a badge of honor signifying a "hard-working" employee.

## The Brain at the Breaking Point

Resilience is the process of adapting well to hardship, trauma, or significant stress. It is the ability to bounce back from challenges and difficulties. Everyone has some resilience, but faced with repeated trauma, our ability to recover from painful experiences can become damaged.

During a crisis, decisions must be made quickly. Normally, our prefrontal cortex, or the thinking brain, handles executive problem solving, organization, emotional regulation, critical thinking, and decision making. However, severe stress leads to significant changes in brain structure and function. This can increase the size of the amygdala, making the brain even more sensitive to stress. Chronic, sustained trauma (much like a pandemic produces) can shrink the prefrontal cortex, the area of the brain responsible for memory and learning. In severe trauma, the hippocampus—the part of the brain responsible for memory recall and differentiating between past and present experiences—can lose volume due to elevated stress hormones. In other words, a brain that has been trained to perceive the world through a trauma lens adapts to become even more sensitive to trauma.

> A brain that has been trained to perceive the world through a trauma lens adapts to become even more sensitive to trauma.

As traumatized adults attempt to cope with elevated stress, anxiety, and depression, their behavior might cause children in their lives to experience additional Adverse Childhood Experience (ACEs)—a vicious cycle. Childhood trauma was reaching epidemic proportions even before COVID-19. In a typical class, more than half the students have experienced at least one ACE. On average, over 60% of adults have experienced at least one ACE. At school, ACEs significantly impact young people in at least two areas: academic performance and social relationships.

Not all people will experience a mass disaster situation or respond to one with extreme trauma reactions, but most have experienced sustained trauma during the pandemic and we can all reach the limits of our resilience. We tend to respond to trauma with three steps: anxiety, angst, and anger. This process creates a "faux logic" in which we believe our responses to stressful stimuli are justified. This can lead to overreactions, judging other people's motivations, and the creation of a false sense of self.[2] When the brain has been affected by trauma, this faux logic can feed us inaccurate information and produce counterproductive thoughts and behaviors. Resilience fatigue can set in, diminishing the brain's executive function and our ability to bounce back.

I've experienced this personally. One week in October 2020, more than six months after the pandemic began, I spent three days in back-to-back Zoom calls with teachers and leaders. I'd been working nonstop, finding resources and research to help schools struggling to implement hybrid learning and meeting weekly with educators who felt disappointed, disgusted, tired, and hopeless. After those three days of nonstop Zoom meetings, I hit a wall. When I closed my computer and got up to walk away, my ring light fell over and broke. I burst into tears. I half-heartedly tried to fix it, but finally threw it across the room. To be honest, in that moment it did me far more good to finish destroying my favorite lamp than to find a way to fix it. After that catharsis, however, I also knew I needed to find a way to work sustainably. If I didn't know my own limits, I couldn't expect others to detect them.

Is resilience an inherent quality or a learned skill? It can be both. Everyone has a certain degree of resilience, but this quality can also be strengthened by developing appropriate skills and support structures. To learn more about resilience and post-traumatic growth, it is helpful to step back and look at a roadmap, then consider where on this journey we have the influence to make strategic inputs to our own and others' resilience.

## A Roadmap to Resilience

Resilience refers to the ability to bounce back from a difficult or challenging situation. Post-traumatic growth refers to something more: not merely bouncing back, but becoming stronger because of all you're going through. The following graphic lays out a path of what post-traumatic growth (labeled here as "PTG") looks like.[3] Crisis induces stress. We respond to stress with coping skills, which can be enhanced by personal factors and external factors. The end result is post-traumatic growth.

The Model of Life Crisis

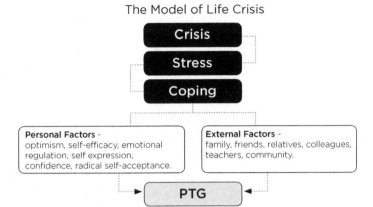

*Adapted from "What Is Post-Traumatic Growth?" from PositivePsychology.com*

## Problem-Focused and Emotion-Focused Coping Skills

We've discussed throughout the book the characteristics of a traumatic crisis and how the stress reactions it creates hinder the brain's higher reasoning abilities. Coping skills fall into two major categories: problem-focused and emotion-focused approaches. Problem-focused coping means handling stress by facing the issue and taking action to resolve the underlying cause. This approach is par for the course for many leaders, who have years of experience managing people, deploying resources, and working through complex problems. In emotion-focused coping, we concentrate on regulating our feelings about the problem rather than on the problem itself. Leaders who are more problem-focused by nature may struggle with emotion-based coping styles. It may seem ineffective or like a waste of time to worry about your emotions or those of your team when you're in the midst of an all-hands-on-deck emergency; however, taking problem-based approaches without considering the emotional beating we and our team are enduring is a sure way to set ourselves up for resilience fatigue. Effective leaders need to be prepared to take both types of approaches depending on their needs and the needs of their team.

> Taking problem-based approaches without considering the emotional beating we and our team are going through is a sure way to set ourselves up for resilience fatigue.

## VIKTOR FRANKL'S SEARCH FOR MEANING

Born in Vienna in 1905, Viktor Frankl endured intense poverty as a young child during World War I and had to beg for food from farmers. Nonetheless, he applied his brilliant mind to the study of psychology by attending public lectures and corresponding with Sigmund Freud, and had already published his first article and begun giving his own lectures by age 15. As a young adult he organized free youth counseling centers and worked to significantly reduce student suicides.

After the German annexation of Austria in 1938, Frankl and his family were in great danger as Jews living under intensifying Nazi oppression. Then the director of neurology at the Rothschild Hospital, Frankl risked his own life by deliberately misdiagnosing mentally ill Jewish patients to prevent them from being euthanized. In 1940, he was one of the fortunate few to receive an immigration visa to America, but decided to forgo it in order to stay and care for his elderly parents. A year later he married a nurse at the hospital. Tragically, the Nazis forced the couple to abort their first child.

In 1942 the family was deported to a Jewish ghetto near Prague, where Frankl's father died of exhaustion within six months. Together with Regina Jones, the world's first female rabbi, Frankl organized a first response team to serve traumatized new arrivals to the camp and prevent suicides. Two years later, the surviving Frankl family members were transferred to Auschwitz-Birkenau, where Viktor's mother was immediately sent to the gas chamber. Frankl's wife and brother were transferred to Bergen-Belsen, where they were both murdered as well.

Frankl survived the war with deep grief over his losses but found consolation in relationships with friends and his passion to write what he had learned for the benefit of others. Over a long postwar career as an acclaimed academic, he authored 39 books, the most famous of which was the autobiographical *Man's Search for Meaning*.

Frankl's thought developed into a new school of therapy known as "logotherapy," classified as a form of existentialism. His core insight was that the main motivation of human beings is to find meaning through the things we do, through the beauty of art, love, etc., or through suffering. When we cannot find meaning, we obsess over experiencing pleasure or exercising power, or we languish in boredom.[5]

Fortunately most people have not endured the deprivations Viktor Frankl did, but millions have found his insights helpful in navigating not only the anguish of suffering, but also the ennui of living comfortable but boring and meaningless lives.

Warren, a school leader I work with closely, spent two weeks during the pandemic just checking in with the staff. Although he was normally a problem-focused leader, he understood how crucial emotion-based coping skills would be to developing and maintaining the resilience of his staff. He started with regular "town halls" where he could convey to the staff the latest information he had, then began holding bimonthly chats with small groups. He kept these positive and upbeat, often beginning the conversation by asking group members to share anything funny that had happened that week. After allowing everyone to share how they were feeling and conveying any information he needed to, Warren ended each meeting with positive affirmations or a good word for the staff. Busy as they were, teachers actually began to request more training sessions and more teachers asked to be part of Warren's cohort groups. They were ready to grow!

## Personal Factors Affecting Coping Skills

The "Personal Factors" designated on our roadmap are the areas where we are most able to grow our own coping skills. These areas include maintaining a sense of optimism, self-efficacy, and emotional regulation; increasing our ability to express ourselves; operating with confidence; and practicing a radical sense of self-acceptance based on our inherent worth as people, not our performance.

The following are some suggested targets for growth in our personal coping skills—areas in which even the best of us can show continual improvement:

> The power of a reframed mindset is not that it minimizes trauma, but that it allows us to reframe the story in a more beneficial way.

1. **A reframed mindset:** To prevent becoming stuck in trauma, we need to visualize a more empathetic future, a future where we're doing more than surviving, but progressing toward a mission that matters. We have to find ways to let go of our disappointment when we've gotten off track, comfort ourselves with closure rituals, and develop healthy and productive protocols to keep moving purposefully forward. We

must, however, avoid toxic positivity—where legitimate concerns are minimized or dismissed. We need to substitute the brutally honest optimism that validates the real struggle we are experiencing but also provides hope. As Viktor Frankl wrote, "Everything can be taken from a man but one thing; the last of the human freedoms—to choose one's attitude in any given set of circumstances, to choose one's own way." The power of a reframed mindset is not that it minimizes trauma, but that it allows us to reframe the story in a more beneficial way.

In *Making Hope Happen*, Shane Lopez offers three elements for a reframed mindset.

- **Goals:** You need to have a future that fires you up!

- **Agency:** You need to believe that you have the power to make that future a reality.

- **Pathways:** You need to know that there are many ways to reach your goal (a.k.a. to go from "here to there") and that none of those paths will be free of obstacles.[6]

> "Everything can be taken from a man but one thing; the last of the human freedoms—to choose one's attitude in any given set of circumstances, to choose one's own way." – Viktor Frankl

2. **Playing to our strengths:** Next, drawing from our reframed mindset, we need to determine what our strengths are and how these can be deployed most effectively. If we have trouble seeing our own strengths, we can think about situations in the past that had positive outcomes and recall our role in them, and the various actions we took that helped produce those results. It can also be extremely helpful to talk to a friend or have a small group share what they have seen as our strengths. These conversations are not fishing for compliments; they are vitally important in helping us identify strengths we may have ignored in ourselves that others see as valuable and even extraordinary gifts.

3. **Rely on a circle of five:** People overcome trauma through supportive and trusted relationships. We would all benefit from knowing five people who will tell us our strengths—and our weaknesses—especially if they can share with us in such a way that we can hear and benefit from

their words. These are the people we can call at 2 a.m. if we're in crisis. At least one of these five should be someone from work. If you can't think of a work friend like that, cultivating one should become a high priority.

4. **Sleep and physical wellness:** Highly productive people in the midst of crisis often put in long hours. We may think we're only temporarily putting aside our needs for sleep, a healthy diet, and exercise, but before we know it we've established poor habits that in the long run will rob us of our time, health, and productivity. Building white space into our calendars for self-care is not a luxury, it's a necessity.

5. **Seek meaning and purpose:** People need to know their "who." We start to find our purpose as we discover who we are and who we connect with. Many of us find meaning through faith, family, and freedoms— enduring concepts that are bigger than ourselves, and that will live on after we are gone. Although these help in discovering meaning and purpose, becoming the best version of ourselves requires that we first know our "who." As Viktor Frankl said, "Man's main concern is not to gain pleasure or to avoid pain but rather to see a meaning in his life."

> "Man's main concern is not to gain pleasure or to avoid pain but rather to see a meaning in his life."
> - Viktor Frankl

6. **Celebrate daily progress:** I recently expanded my to-do list to include things I'm grateful for and concerned about, not just tasks to check off. Not everyone is a "list person," but keeping some kind of record not only of things we have to do but also the progress we make can help generate and maintain our momentum. Alternatives to making a list include journaling or making a private video diary, just a minute a day. Taking time to acknowledge daily progress is imperative to post-traumatic growth.

## External Factors Affecting Resilience

The influence of family, friends, colleagues, authority figures, and the community are external factors that can affect our resilience. Another external factor is the physical environment we find ourselves in or create for ourselves. At an individual level, we all have at least some influence over our external environment. We can't choose our family, but we can choose how much we allow them to be part of our lives. For our own good, it might be time to put distance in some of those relationships, or sever them altogether. Even in a toxic workplace, we can take some control over our physical workspace to make it warm and encouraging. We can also gather the courage to speak up and set boundaries with those who make our work experience difficult. Ultimately, we could change our work environment by seeking a different job.

Educational leaders must reflect on how to become a positive external influence. Competent, high-functioning teammates can become resources who help one another through struggles. To be a positive external influence in the lives of others—friends, family, colleagues, and our students—we can consider:

- Being an active listener. Set everything else aside, make eye contact, and give full attention.

- Finding points of commonality, letting the other person know they are not the only one who feels this way.

- Genuinely getting to know other people and what they need, not just what we want to give them.

- Observing others' strengths, catching them doing something well, and pointing it out.

- "Sandwiching" necessary constructive criticism between statements of genuine, meaningful praise and affirmation. This humanizing practice helps to strengthen relationships, and when we practice the habit of delivering feedback in this format, it becomes second nature.

Our ability to affect the physical environment of other adults who are not under our authority is more limited, but we can certainly invite them to a space that might stimulate positivity and creativity.

We have even more influence within a classroom to strengthen resilience with a thoughtfully planned physical environment. Most teachers take advantage of the opportunity to decorate their rooms with cheerful and inspiring art or manipulate the arrangement of chairs to facilitate group learning. Some create work stations or quiet areas where stressed students can get some time apart from the group to calm down and recharge. Teachers can be mindful of different learning styles when considering their design. Some students may be distracted by a room where every wall is a riot of color and activity, while others may get bored by a minimalist aesthetic. Giving students some agency to arrange their seats in groups facing different directions, with one side of the room more exciting and the other more calming, might be a solution.

Classrooms also can be specifically designed to support traumatized students. The principles of trauma-informed design include creating an engaging multisensory experience, providing connection to the natural world, creating separation from those who are in distress, reinforcing personal identity and self-reliance, and creating the opportunity for choice. All this must be done, of course, while also considering the needs and comfort of the majority.[7]

Seating arrangements are one important example of the special requirements of children who have been through trauma. The right seating arrangement can contribute to a student's ability to show resilience after a difficult circumstance or ongoing stress, while the wrong seating arrangement can have the opposite effect. Many times when students struggle, they are placed in closer proximity to the teacher—often at the front of the room. For students with trauma, this can be disastrous. They are used to being constantly on high alert, keeping themselves feeling safe through hyper-awareness of their surroundings. Placing a traumatized student with his back to others or the door can trigger the amygdala with danger signals without giving the student the ability to fight, flee, or freeze, at least not without it negatively affecting the student or the class. At the very least, they will find it difficult to stay focused, and their academic performance may fall still further.

Whether renovating or building new, facilities can be a part of a comprehensive solution. At a middle school in an inner-city area, one campus had struggled for years with discipline, academic gaps, and future-ready skills. The campus was finally upgraded from its early 1930s facility to a vibrant, dynamic, collaborative space. The leadership worked with staff to create systems, structures, and instructional strategies to prepare for the new space, and to help the staff understand why this large-scale change would benefit their students. The reaction of the students and the surrounding community to the new campus was overwhelming and surprisingly positive. Community pride reached an all-time high. One student said, "I feel like I don't go to the ghetto school anymore. It's like we matter." The environment is never neutral. It either inhibits or enhances resilience. It either helps or hinders growing within trauma.

**"THREE PRACTICES THAT SET RESILIENT TEAMS APART"**[8]

Keith Ferrazzi and CeCe Morken, authors of *Competing in the World of Work*, conducted research on 272 global businesses to discover practices that built resilience into their employees. They found that a major contributing factor to resilience is high-functioning teamwork. Specifically, they were able to identify three easily executable practices of successful teams that can re-energize resilience:

- **Resilient teams limit unnecessary meetings.** Excessive meetings waste time and energy and decrease productivity. Asynchronous collaboration gives people more time to think about their responses and opens participation to more individuals, increasing the potential for creative solutions.

- **Resilient teams build supportive relationships.** The team develops a culture that is supportive of members reaching out to one another and sharing their personal and professional struggles. People need to feel cared for as individuals, not be treated like cogs in a wheel.

- **Resilient teams work to enhance one another's energy and wellness.** Team members realize that success depends upon every member of the group functioning at their best. Members are encouraged to share with one another what may be sapping their energy, and teammates may help relieve the areas of stress by redistributing the workload.

## What Does Post-Traumatic Growth Look Like?

The last part of our diagram is, of course, post-traumatic growth. What does that look like? Post-traumatic growth starts with acceptance and positive reinterpretation: We have to accept the situation as it is, rather than fruitlessly raging that it is not the way we want it to be. When we practice positive reinterpretation, we seek out the positive aspects of the situation and find meaning in the experience. This can be difficult to model when we're in a serious crisis, but leaders who are able to do so with finesse will find their influence greatly expanded in an environment where such desirable qualities are in short supply.

Post-traumatic growth will look different for each person, but here are examples from the field of how we might see it in our schools, demonstrating each of the five domains of post-traumatic growth:

1. **Personal strength:** Greater feeling of self-reliance, recognition of one's ability to handle challenges; a discovery of being stronger than we thought we were. Staff and students move from doubting their ability toward feeling like they can. One teacher, Nancy, reports,

   I had never used technology in my classroom. In fact, I didn't even have a computer in my home before the shutdown! I'm only five years away from retirement so honestly, I thought I could avoid it. But after we got some training on gamification, I tried it in hybrid instruction and my students loved it. I guess you can teach an old dog new tricks.

2. **Closer relationships:** More openness to sharing with others about our struggles and a willingness to reach out and rely upon others for help when we need it. Increased compassion for those who suffer and more effort put into relationships. Movement from distant relationships to deeper engagement with others. Judy, a middle school principal, describes what this looks like at her school:

   There was a lot of competition between our teachers at the same grade level. In response we worked on collaboration, including building in longer collaborative planning periods. One caveat was that the teachers at each grade level had to touch base with each other and me in virtual meetings weekly for a wellness check. We built trust by taking turns sharing stories of how COVID affected someone in our school community, and we'd always share a fun tidbit or even recipes. The teachers began finding a camaraderie we didn't have before. The competition has turned into a more collaborative conversation. One grade level had two teachers who had previously requested transfers. They canceled them because they have "grown to love the team"—their words, not mine!

3. **Greater appreciation of life:** A changed sense of priorities about what is important. An increase in valuing the importance of "little things" or things formerly taken for granted. Gratitude comes with more presence and mindfulness. Movement from resentment or bitterness toward gratitude. Sherri says,

I was a workhorse at home and school. I wanted to get there, buckle down, and get moving. As a leader, I was there early and busy all day. It always bothered me when people just wanted to come chitchat because it just put me behind. I have two children, a husband who works out of town, and elderly parents. My mother got COVID and passed away when we were trying to get everyone online for instruction right after COVID hit. I remember the last time I talked to my mother. I went by and talked to her through the door. She said, "Michelle, can you just sit?" I told her no—I was too busy taking care of everything. That was the last time I communicated with my mother. That changed me. I am grateful for the gift of my family and health more than ever. I am less hurried and spend more time with people. One of the staff members mentioned the other day that before I looked like I was always running late to a meeting. She said since we'd returned, the little things and words of encouragement made them all feel valued. It hit me that before I was just running a school, and now I'm actually leading one.

4. **A vision for new possibilities:** We become more likely to change things that need changing. We have a willingness to explore opportunities we never considered before. We accept the breakage and become more open to new ways of living. We recognize new opportunities. This is a movement from a survivor mindset to a thriver mindset. Jen describes it like this:

> As an instructional leader, I worked diligently with a teacher to move her toward more student-centered instruction. I'd brought in training, coaching, you name it but it never clicked. She was resistant to having students talk and was stuck in a cycle of lecture and assessment. During virtual instruction, the lack of engagement of her students was palpable. They wouldn't turn on their cameras. It alarmed her. She finally asked why and one brave student replied, "All we do is listen to you lecture and now the notes are online. Does it matter if you see me listen?" It hit her like a ton of bricks. She could have punished the student but instead became reflective. She reached out to the trainers and came up with some things to help her engage students in the lessons. When we were back on-site for instruction, she kept these practices up. I had walk-throughs of classrooms with some other leaders. To my surprise, in her room students were

collaborating and writing information on the community writable surfaces. It was a night and day difference. When I praised her efforts, she said, "I knew that we were moving this direction but never saw the need until now. I would never go back."

5. **Spiritual development or change:** We experience life at a deeper level of awareness. We develop a sense of spirituality and meaning. Growth is experienced through engaging a greater cognitive existential quest. We experience movement from feelings of hopelessness to contentment. Justin, an elementary school music teacher, shares the following:

> I began to realize that my level of control was much less than I realized. I could focus on what I could control but some things I had to let go of. I began to search for more clarity and a larger purpose. When I found it, I began to realize the behaviors I had been modeling weren't helping any of those around me. In fact, I was contributing to their anxiety and discontentment. I found a renewed faith, which gave me some comfort and connection. My faith in God has deepened and I wouldn't make it through these days without Him.

Nelson Mandela said, "I never lose. I either win or learn." From the lens of a growth mindset, every failure is a chance to get better. It's not win or lose. It's about incremental improvement. That is why building a culture and climate that honors growth is crucial. There is no magic potion or silver bullet, but there is something better: When we develop resilience in our team members, they can help fill in the cracks in our fractured world. Moving toward resilience gives people more capacity to come together instead of being driven apart. With thoughtful, engaged, well-informed leadership, our teams can move past fear and into the freedom to create a future of resilient individuals ready to face the challenges that will come.

## SURVIVING THE STORM

### REFLECTION QUESTIONS

1. If you were to rate your level of resilience right now, would you describe yourself as being close to "resilience fatigue"? What practical steps will you take to improve your resilience?

2. Considering the giftedness of your team, as a group are you stronger in problem-focused or emotion-focused coping skills?

3. What personal factors are strengths in your resilience? What personal factors interfere with your resilience? How can you improve these?

4. In your classroom or your team, what are some simple changes you can make to improve external factors that will contribute to the group's resilience?

### STRAIGHTFORWARD SURVIVAL

When we experience disruption, sometimes we need simple ideas for taking a next, practical step forward. If you are unsure of where to start, choose one of these ideas from the chapter:

- Celebrate and be grateful for daily accomplishments.

- Implement a personal/professional check-in at the beginning of meetings or phone calls and discuss struggles and celebrations.

- Plan time together with someone in your "circle of five"—the five people you can talk to about your strengths and weaknesses.

## ENDNOTES

1. S. Vozza, (2022, March 10), "5 Subtle Signs You're Headed for Burnout," *Fast Company*. Retrieved April 4, 2022, from https://www.fastcompany.com/90727550/5-subtle-signs-youre-headed-for-burnout.

2. R. Miller, et al., (2020), *Whole: What Teachers Need to Help Students Thrive*. Jossey-Bass.

3. R. Hudgens, et al., (2020, September 1), "Helping You Help Others," *Positive Psychology*. Retrieved March 28, 2022, from https://positivepsychology.com/post-traumatic-growth/.

4. "Viktor Emil Frankl," (n.d.), *Viktor Frankl Institut*. Retrieved April 19, 2022, from https://www.univie.ac.at/logotherapy/biography.html.

5. "Who Was Viktor Frankl?" (2022), *Pursuit of Happiness*. Retrieved from https://www.pursuit-of-happiness.org/history-of-happiness/viktor-frankl/.

6. S. Lopez, (2014), *Making Hope Happen: Create the Future You Want for Yourself and Others*. Atria.

7. N. Gill, (2019, December 9), "Council Post: The Importance of Trauma-Informed Design." *Forbes*. Retrieved March 29, 2022, from https://www.forbes.com/sites/forbesnonprofitcouncil/2019/12/09/the-importance-of-trauma-informed-design.

8. K. Ferrazzi and C. C. Morken, (2022, March 17), "3 Practices That Set Resilient Teams Apart," *Harvard Business Review*. Retrieved April 4, 2022, from https://hbr.org/2022/03/3-practices-that-set-resilient-teams-apart.

# CHAPTER 5: RESTORING CONFIDENCE
## Getting Back on Our Feet and Moving Forward

*"I'll always work hard and do my best, but I don't expect anything in return . . . I know my happiness doesn't depend on it anymore."*[1]

Record-shattering big wave surfer Maya Gabeira spoke these words as she recalled being slammed by an 80-foot wave in the world-famous surf of Nazaré, Portugal. The derailing crash upended her surfing goals and left her with serious injuries—and could have taken her life. Though the context is quite different, her words echo the deep wisdom of Austrian neurologist and concentration camp survivor Viktor Frankl. As we saw in the last chapter, Frankl learned from the heartbreaking losses of his life that in the midst of our deepest difficulties and traumas, we can continue to find meaning and purpose if we devote ourselves to a cause greater than ourselves. As he said,

> Don't aim at success. The more you aim at it and make it a target, the more you are going to miss it. For success, like happiness, cannot be pursued; it must ensue, and it only does so as the unintended side effect of one's personal dedication to a cause greater than oneself or as the by-product of one's surrender to a person other than oneself. Happiness must happen, and the same holds for success: you have to let it happen by not caring about it. I want you to listen to what your conscience commands you to do and go on to carry it out to the best of your knowledge. Then you will live to see that in the long run—in the long run, I say!—success will follow you precisely because you had forgotten to think about it.[2]

## SURVIVING THE STORM

We can't work to create our own happiness, Frankl seems to say—but our confidence and even our happiness can grow out of our commitment to the meaningful calling we pursue. When someone suffers a trauma, their confidence can be crushed, particularly if they tied their future happiness to the achievement of a particular goal or set of events. But if instead the focus is on the daily process of "listening to what your conscience demands and carrying it out" versus striving for specific results, confidence, and often happiness, will result—even in the midst of crushing defeats.

Gabeira experienced crushing defeat in that life-altering crash. Dropping into an immense wave at nearly 40 miles per hour, she lost balance, broke her fibula, fell, and popped back to the surface just in time to see a literal ocean of water crash down on her. Her life jacket was torn away and she tumbled through the water, unable to tell which way was up. Her partner was on a jet ski and managed to drag Maya to shore, where the lifeguard administered CPR to restore her to consciousness. After two back surgeries and 18 grueling months of physical therapy, she was derailed and injured, but ultimately not deterred. She continues to shatter records and push the boundaries of big wave surfing.[3] "It humbled me a lot," says Gabeira. "It showed me how much I didn't have everything under control and organized, and how much more I had to improve. But more than that, it really detached me from achievements—which is funny, because then I did get two world records after it ... but that was never the priority."[4]

## KNOCKED OFF BALANCE

Sometimes people find it difficult to identify with those who suffer, especially when, with the benefit of hindsight, we can point out where their decision-making went wrong or what additional precautions we would have taken. Not all of us, for instance, will understand the reasoning of participating in a high-risk sport like Gabeira's. The COVID pandemic, however, has broadened our understanding of suffering. It's never been clearer how susceptible each one of us is to circumstances outside of ourselves. We are no longer unaware of how an unstoppable crisis can impact and derail us, both individually and collectively. We have been through a communal traumatic experience.

Many of us have lost confidence in the face of this collective crisis. To move forward, we not only need to rebuild that confidence to what it was before, but to seek something more than what we previously had. We need to use all that we have lost and learned over the past years and let it lead us to post-traumatic growth.

The concept of regaining confidence is closely related to efficacy—the belief that we have the ability to complete a task, alone or as a group. For educators, confidence is the strength of that belief in ourselves and our schools. In post-traumatic recovery, not only do we realize we can do it, but we also make a courageous decision that we will do it.

> In post-traumatic recovery, not only do we realize we can do it, but we also make a courageous decision that we will do it.

## A Crisis of Confidence

In 1976 President Jimmy Carter gave a historic speech in which he spoke of something we can relate to today—a "crisis of confidence." As the country struggled with high inflation, weak economic growth, and foreign policy setbacks, an exhausted population felt the country lacked direction and purpose. On top of it all the nation was gripped with news of the Iranian Hostage Crisis, a source of palpable stress. Americans were increasingly unwilling to cooperate with government institutions that seemed unable to solve problems effectively—yet many of these problems were so large they could not be solved by individuals or the private sector. Feeling powerless and directionless, most people concerned themselves with their personal issues and disengaged from the community.

Disrupted confidence is not always directed inward. We can know full well that we have what it takes to handle the challenges in our lives, yet can feel a lack of confidence in our leaders and the direction in which they are trying to take us. When we feel trapped in a larger system that puts limits on what we can do, we stop trying. At times this is a perfectly rational decision that conserves our energy.

## CRISIS OF CONFIDENCE

This is an excerpt from a 1976 speech by President Carter describing a "crisis of confidence" in the country.

The threat is nearly invisible in ordinary ways. It is a crisis of confidence. It is a crisis that strikes at the very heart and soul and spirit of our national will. We can see this crisis in the growing doubt about the meaning of our own lives and in the loss of a unity of purpose for our nation.

The erosion of our confidence in the future is threatening to destroy the social and the political fabric of America.

The confidence that we have always had as a people is not simply some romantic dream or a proverb in a dusty book that we read just on the Fourth of July.

It is the idea which founded our nation and has guided our development as a people. Confidence in the future has supported everything else— public institutions and private enterprise, our own families, and the very Constitution of the United States. Confidence has defined our course and has served as a link between generations. We've always believed in something called progress. We've always had a faith that the days of our children would be better than our own.

Our people are losing that faith, not only in government itself but in the ability as citizens to serve as the ultimate rulers and shapers of our democracy. As a people we know our past and we are proud of it. Our progress has been part of the living history of America, even the world. We always believed that we were part of a great movement of humanity itself called democracy, involved in the search for freedom, and that belief has always strengthened us in our purpose. But just as we are losing our confidence in the future, we are also beginning to close the door on our past.

In a nation that was proud of hard work, strong families, close-knit communities, and our faith in God, too many of us now tend to worship self-indulgence and consumption. Human identity is no longer defined by what one does, but by what one owns. But we've discovered that owning things and consuming things does not satisfy our longing for meaning. We've learned that piling up material goods cannot fill the emptiness of lives which have no confidence or purpose. The symptoms of this crisis of the American spirit are all around us.[5]

In March of 2021, I taught a seminar for administrators on post-traumatic growth and the crisis of confidence in our schools. I did an informal survey, asking the audience to choose the statement that best describes how they felt at that time.

- 5% chose "Making it one day at a time!"
- 7% chose "Different day, different hat!"
- 18% chose "One of me, many of you!"
- 70% chose "Looking at my options . . . how far away is retirement?"

I offered the last option tongue-in-cheek, but it turned out to be no joke. A year into the pandemic, the vast majority of my audience felt ready to quit their jobs. Scientific polling bears out this anecdotal observation. A survey of over 500 secondary school principals conducted in the fall of 2021 found that 40% expected to quit their job within three years; 30% said they would leave education altogether as soon as they could land a better-paying job.[6]

When schools first shut down, teachers became heroes of the community. Many parents voiced appreciation of their hard work. Communities banded together to help in any way they could. Then, the narrative changed. Uncertainty grew. Weary and disillusioned members of the community began to stir up dissension. Teachers came under more scrutiny than ever before. It was as if a nameless, faceless force had punctured holes in the "can-do" community spirit that had buoyed us through the first wave of the pandemic, leaving us sinking and squabbling as more waves loomed. Educators and administrators are exhausted. We are at a point when many of them are leaving the profession, not only due to the pressures of the pandemic, but also because of long-term systemic problems including social issues resulting from inequity; lack of resources; the necessity of mastering new technology and helping their students do so; political pressure in the community over every aspect of education; and sheer stress and burnout. Much like Vietnam Vets returning from the war, educators are experiencing long-term first responder fatigue with no prospect of it ending, even when the immediate crisis has passed.

---

### EDUCATION IS A HABITAT FOR HEROES

"Education is a habitat for heroes. And, what else would we expect? Teaching tackles and fulfills one of the most foundational and primordial purposes of civilization. Teachers prepare children for adulthood and careers. More than that, they preserve the social order. That very milieu attracts those of heroic spirit. That heroic dimension is why teaching provides an exceptional and recurrent focus for books and movies. Each generation of teachers can point to a printed or filmed story of heroes–*Up the Down Staircase, Stand and Deliver, Mr. Holland's Opus, Dead Poet's Society, Goodbye, Mr. Chips*, etc. Each spoke to the hero's heart in millions of boys or girls, sitting in movie theaters or curled up in Dad's reading chair."[7]

---

## REBUILDING INSTITUTIONAL CONFIDENCE

We've seen so far that the forces of chaos can disrupt our personal confidence and our confidence in institutions. Our educational system has been in crisis for decades, causing teacher burnout even before the waves of COVID-19 crashed on us. In pandemic conditions, administrators have looked for technological fixes that have too often created more work for teachers, rather than giving them the one thing they say they need most: time. Due to personnel and resource shortages, more time isn't available to us.

With this as our reality, we must come to grips with the fact that the band-aids we have put on these problems to survive the pandemic are not going to help long-term. There is no going back to the normal of pre-pandemic life. The systemic issues in education that were crippling us are still here, demanding fundamental reform that will create a viable, sustainable, 21st-century educational system. That being said, we have to function in the world as it is, not as we hope and plan for it to be one day. At the level of individual teachers and administrators, our ability to effect broad institutional change is limited. However, each of us can play a role in building trust, communicating, connecting, and collaborating in such a way that we rebuild confidence in ourselves, our schools, and our communities.

One way to rebuild that confidence is by assessing our school communities through a "4M" framework, looking at the Micro, Meso, Macro, and Mega levels. The 4M framework was informed by what's known as systems theory. Systems theory was developed within the Scholarship of Teaching and Learning (SoTL) community to help educators understand teaching and learning inquiry.[8] We are going to modify the framework for school leadership, focusing on the issue of building confidence at all levels of the school community. When we do so, we'll find that we have resources and opportunities available at each level that will allow us to rebuild disrupted confidence.

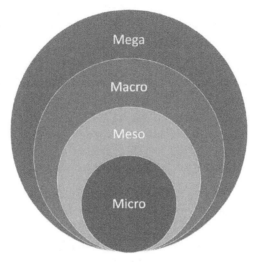

*The 4M Framework. Image recreated based on content found at https://drsaraheaton.wordpress.com/tag/4m-framework/.*

### 1. The Micro Level: The Individual

We have the most daily contact with, and influence over, individuals. Keeping our fingers on the pulse of this group is critical. It is much easier to influence a potential problem in a positive way as it develops than it is to deal with a train wreck that's out of control. On the minus side, this group notices inequities quickly, especially if they feel slighted. Our response is critical to developing confidence. Thoughts to reflect upon:

- **Be present:** On the Micro level, simple ways to build confidence are visiting classrooms, talking to students, going to recess, and being in the cafeteria. An administrator recently shared with me that checking in with students and staff every morning was the single most valuable action she took each day. If it's a disruption when you poke your head in the classroom, you likely haven't been present enough. Make it such a regular occurrence students and faculty see it as normal.

- **Be available:** Keep time in your schedule to meet with teachers. Don't give them the feeling that you're too busy to hear their concerns. When you are tied up and cannot meet with them immediately, put a high priority on following up the moment you become free.

- **Be trustworthy:** If you say you are going to do something, do it. Don't give due dates that are not feasible for yourself or your teachers. If you struggle with organization and things fall through the cracks, use a to-do list or set a reminder on your phone.

- **Leave tangible affirmations:** I bring a bright pink pad of sticky notes when I visit campuses so I can jot down a quick note to leave for a teacher: maybe something funny the teacher or a student said, or an observation of something I saw a child working on. It just needs to be positive and intentional. Never leave a message that says, "Come see me." This phrase is the quickest way to ruin a teacher's day—or anyone else's, for that matter.

> Never leave a message that says, "Come see me." It's the quickest way to ruin a teacher's day—or anyone else's, for that matter.

## 2. The Meso Level: The Department or Grade

Departments are the Meso level for school districts. In schools, content or grade levels represent the Meso level. This is the level that may have the greatest impact on students' academic success. The people involved at the Meso level can be an excellent pool for recruiting and developing leaders. However, this is also a level that can become territorial and siloed. Giving individuals a broader view of the needs of other departments and how they fit into the strategy of the organization as a whole is critical. Thoughts to reflect upon:

- **Set expectations:** To break down silos, leaders must provide a framework and set expectations for various groups to work together. Consider a 3:1 ratio of meetings with support staff, inviting them to one out of every three grade or content area meetings. If a leader is aware of impending issues or concerns, they should proactively attend related meetings at the Meso level to stay on top of developing issues before they get heated.

- **Include "orphaned" programs:** Not all programs of the school or district fit neatly into the existing administrative structure. However, those who work in these programs may be uniquely positioned to see the perspectives of more than one department. They can often be quite helpful in providing unique input and ideas.

- **Celebrate team wins:** Learning to work across silos is a new skill in many institutions and can be especially challenging for individuals with disrupted confidence. Try to catch people and groups engaging in the behaviors we're trying to reinforce. Highlight collaboration efforts and any positive results from them to encourage others to follow their example.

3. **The Macro Level: The Organization**

The Macro level describes the system as a whole. It's possible for individuals and even whole departments to function confidently within an organization while the institution as a whole may not enjoy the confidence of its constituents. Thoughts to reflect upon:

- **Ensure equity:** Campus leaders still represent the district, and district leaders need to look out for campuses. At all levels we need to pay attention to needs and strive for a strategically balanced allocation of resources. Even if an identified problem cannot be resolved immediately, those affected will likely feel somewhat satisfied that progress is being made as long as they know the issue is not being ignored. All groups should feel equally important and valued, even if not all of their needs can be addressed at the same time.

- **Leadership summits:** Quarterly leadership summits are a great way to bring campus and district leaders together to learn new information and brainstorm applications for it. Keep in mind as you plan these summits that the number one perceived need of teachers is more time. We have to make sure these meetings are not just pro forma, but that they genuinely bring value—new ideas, strategies, or processes that will be practical and impactful. When planned thoughtfully, these summits will go a long way toward fostering alignment and building confidence.

- **Communicate regularly:** Regular communication from leaders to all levels of the organization is important not only to provide valuable information to the whole staff, but to recognize and celebrate successes and to create a sense of connection between the staff and the leadership. Consider creating one-minute video "commercials" with the important points summarized in an email to give a busy audience more than one way to access the information.

4. **The Mega Level: The Community**

The Mega level represents the entire school community in the broadest sense, one that includes government bodies, parents, alumni, local businesses, and members of the local community who interact with and support the district. How can we build confidence in our school system within such a broad and diverse group? Thoughts to reflect upon:

- **Communicate judiciously:** This group does not need to know all the intricacies of the new math program your district is implementing, but if they recognize the program's name and have a sense of how it is improving student learning they will feel more connected with and invested in the school community. Educators love words, but when reaching out to the Mega level try to sometimes communicate in more visual ways to reach hearts as well as minds.

- **Address diverse interests:** Let the community know all the schools have to offer that may be of interest to them, including sports, musical and artistic performances, and more. Involving community members in these activities helps create advocates who have confidence in the value the school brings to those beyond students, teachers, and staff.

- **Draw upon problem solvers:** Local businesses can be a wealth of information about what skills and abilities they are looking for in future employees. Regional colleges may be able to share what they've observed of the struggles incoming students are having, and ideas to help prepare students for the transition to higher education. Reaching out to another related institution gives a different purview of the skills needed and provides a fresh lens to foster innovation. Forging these kinds of broader connections can help those outside our own institutions have confidence that the school or district is serious about adequately preparing graduates with real-world skills.

- **Include the excluded:** Who in the community is not participating in or connected with our schools? Investigate the reasons for this so that our schools do not miss out on the contributions of people who may be in a position to make a substantial difference. Including traditionally excluded members of the community builds confidence in the school as a caring institution.

By working at the Micro, Meso, Macro, and Mega levels, we can build a broad base of advocates who have a common cause in supporting our schools despite their other differences. In one school community, very few parents participated in the PTA because they were working during the day at the largest employer in town. Learning of this, Tom, the plant manager of that large employer, arranged for parents to take time off work if they wished to attend PTA meetings. Tom was invited to visit a local school. He couldn't believe the poor shape of the school's media centers, so he took the initiative to approach his CEO as well as other businesses and foundations, successfully gathering resources to equip two schools with state-of-the-art media centers that aligned with their needs. Through these community connections, the area schools won the confidence of a Mega-level advocate who facilitated more parent participation, as well as substantial resources in a badly neglected area of their work.

As we think about the 4M framework and use it to redevelop confidence, we must keep in mind the importance of matching the size of the problem with the appropriate level of the framework. Many times, we take problems that the Micro level could address into a Mega group. This only frustrates participants and slows or stops the progress toward a solution, eroding institutional confidence all along the way. Micro problems shouldn't be solved in a public (Mega) arena. When approaching a problem, think about which group has the ability to effectively solve that issue.

## REBUILDING PERSONAL CONFIDENCE

We don't always find ourselves in institutions that have the resources, will, or vision to make broad transformative changes. And let's be honest— some workplaces are just plain toxic. Even though there are many job openings for educators, individuals in an unsupportive environment may not be at a place in life where they can consider relocating for a better job. How can we rebuild our personal confidence as professionals, even if our external circumstances are not ideal?

Most teachers in the trenches do not need esoteric ideas about educational reform—they need practical ideas to survive in their profession today. A professional with a sense of efficacy is not rattled when they don't succeed at a task; that experience simply pinpoints a particular skill they need to develop, and they set about doing so. Sometimes, though, faced with difficult situations, we internalize a sense of shame. Brené Brown explains it this way: "Shame is 'I am bad.' Guilt is 'I did something bad.'" Disrupted confidence can be closely related to shame. It's about whether or not you put faith in yourself as a good, worthy person. Efficacy is the faith you have in your ability to complete a task. Confidence is the faith you have in yourself. How do we rebuild our personal confidence when the waves keep knocking us down and help may not be forthcoming? Here are a few ideas to consider:

1. **Find your "who":** Confidence isn't based on what a person does or their accomplishments. Confidence, rather, is tied to understanding your purpose, and purpose comes out of an innate sense of knowing who you are. According to psychologist Abraham Maslow, each of us has an inner sense of our own potential. Every one of us should ask ourselves, How can I become the best version of myself under any conditions? Where can I use my best to serve others? And how can I close the gap between what I could be and what I am?

2. **Set realistic goals:** Confidence is not about having all the answers, it's about believing that we will be able to find the answers we need. We can set future goals that are in that sweet spot of "challenging but not impossible." We can't slay every dragon at once, but we can tackle one at a time and build momentum from there.

3. **Address the stress:** Self-reflection is a huge piece of growing and building confidence. What responsibilities and expectations are we placing on ourselves? Are these things under our control? Did someone else place them in our backpack or did we put them there ourselves? Which responsibilities and expectations can we throw away? Sometimes "good enough" is actually good enough.

> Sometimes 'good enough' is actually good enough.

4. **Increase stamina.** We can prioritize a few important tasks each day, working in spurts of 25 minutes punctuated by five-minute breaks (the Pomodoro Method), and periodically taking longer breaks or a power nap to recover and reset our energy and motivation. If a break recharges you so you can get twice as much work done twice

as efficiently, then think of taking breaks like eating or drinking—you can't afford not to do it. It's also critically important to prioritize rest in ourselves and in those on our teams. "The lack of quality sleep builds a logjam of mental and physical health issues. That's why improving sleep forms the single most effective way to lower stress and improve health."[9]

## Confidently Facing the Future

A lot has happened to sap our confidence in ourselves and in the institutions we serve, but we shouldn't forget how many things we have going for us as we move forward:

- Education is being funded like never before.

- Technology has moved from being a toy to being a tool.

- More attention is being paid to wellness and trauma.

- We're beginning to strip away what is superfluous and ineffective.

- We have a front-row seat to an unprecedented reinvention of the way we do education.

Ashley Chohlis, an executive director of student and community engagement, came through the pandemic with such a vision:

> I'm more confident in my leadership skills today because of the pandemic. Going through hard things makes us stronger. Having to rely on each other during uncertain times made our team stronger too. I believe public education is more adaptable now. The pandemic really showed us what we're capable of providing students when options are limited. Now that we're back in school, I think it gives us options and new skills to enrich our previous approaches.[10]

School leaders have serious choices to make. We can languish, waiting for things to get to some semblance of the normal we once knew (and to be honest, were not very satisfied with). We can play it safe, do what it takes to survive, not expect much, and disengage. We can stay stuck in a limited vision that looks more to the past than the future.

Or, we can lead. Playing it safe does not build confidence—taking risks does. We can dare to dream and do mighty things, things we've always wanted to try but couldn't in a system that was stuck. We can watch for those signs of hope that will inevitably come. Every school can and will experience a tangible turning of the corner, and we have to keep our eyes open for these markers, acknowledge them, and call others' attention to them, too. As we move ahead we will try, fail, try again, fail, and keep trying as we forge a new path. And as we go, we can provide emotional, social, physical, and intellectual safety for our students and teachers. We can coach, support, and push ourselves and those under our influence toward a future we will prefer over a lost past. We have little to lose, and much to gain.

## REFLECTION QUESTIONS

1. In what areas have you experienced a crisis of confidence over the past couple of years?

2. In your relationships, what are specific things you might do at the Micro, Meso, Macro, and Mega levels to help restore disrupted confidence?

3. What are some specific ways you have noticed an increase in your own confidence? Have you noticed improvements in any of your other personal strengths?

## STRAIGHTFORWARD SURVIVAL

When we experience disruption, sometimes we need simple ideas for taking a next, practical step forward. If you are unsure of where to start, choose one of these ideas from the chapter:

- Connect with community supporters to help solve problems. Who could you reach out to?

- Provide regular and predictable lines of communication. What are some ways you will consistently communicate each week with staff and the school community?

- Increase stamina by prioritizing a few essential tasks each day, working in spurts of 25 minutes punctuated by five-minute breaks (the Pomodoro Method).

## ENDNOTES

1.  Bried, E. (2015, May 16). What It's Like To Be me: I Was Crushed By an 80-Foot Wave. *Self.* Retrieved March 8, 2022, from https://www.self.com/story/what-its-like-to-be-me-i-was-crushed-by-an-80-foot-wave.

2.  D. Bates, (2019, Oct. 29), "You're Doing Happiness Wrong," *Psychology Today.* Retrieved April 26, 2022 from: https://www.psychologytoday.com/us/blog/mental-health-nerd/201910/youre-doing-happiness-wrong.

3.  Bried, E. (2015, May 16). What It's Like To Be Me: I Was Crushed by an 80-Foot Wave. *Self.* Retrieved March 8, 2022, from https://www.self.com/story/what-its-like-to-be-me-i-was-crushed-by-an-80-foot-wave.

4.  G. Ramsay, (2021, April 27), "How Maya Gabeira Overcame a Life-Threatening Accident to Surf Two Record-Breaking Waves," CNN. Retrieved April 26, 2022, from https://www.cnn.com/2021/04/27/sport/maya-gabeira-big-wave-surfer-spt-intl-cmd/index.html.

5.  Public Broadcasting Service, (n.d.), "Crisis of Confidence." PBS. Retrieved April 14, 2022, from https://www.pbs.org/wgbh/americanexperience/features/carter-crisis/.

6.  M. McMurdock, (2022, February 20), "School Leader Crisis: Overwhelmed by Mounting Mental Health Issues and Public Distrust, a 'Mass Exodus' of Principals Could Be Coming. Retrieved April 4, 2022, from https://www.the74million.org/article/school-leaders-crisis-overwhelmed-by-mounting-mental-health-issues-public-distrust-mass-exodus-of-principals-could-be-coming/.

7.  R. Miller, (2020), *WHOLE: What Teachers Need to Help Students Thrive,* Jossey-Bass.

8.  S.E. Eaton, (n.d.), "4M framework. Learning, Teaching and Leadership." Retrieved April 14, 2022, from https://drsaraheaton.wordpress.com/tag/4m-framework/.

9.  R. Miller and J. Jernigan, (2021). Strategy in Rebuilding: Principles to Building Post-traumatic Growth [PDF]. Retrieved April 20, 2022, from: https://rexmiller.com/shop/ols/products/strategy-in-rebuilding-principles-to-build-post-traumatic-growth.

10. Whorton, L., & The Holdsworth Center. (2022, March 8). Two Years In, Educators Reflect on Pandemic Leadership. The Holdsworth Center. Retrieved April 4, 2022.

# CHAPTER 6: RESTORING CONTROL
## The Limitations and Possibilities of Influence

Unexpected, destructive, and unpredictable: Wildfires are a seasonal scourge in the dry Western States that cost billions of dollars and scores of lives every year. My parents were forced to evacuate when a wildfire threatened their home. Mom's an organized lady. She moved quickly but methodically through the house, grabbing irreplaceable things: her grandmother's quilt, Dad's army jacket, family photos, mementos of my and my brother's childhoods. She packed her belongings in the car as tightly as the pieces in a game of Tetris, leaving just enough space for herself and my dad and the dogs. To our entire family's great relief, the wind changed direction and the fire moved away from the house, but Mom decided to keep all those precious keepsakes in the car anyway, just in case it came back.

When our lives are disrupted, we look for something we can control. In fire season that might mean packing the car or spraying down the yard with a water hose. And once we feel like we have some control, we're reluctant to relinquish it.

Large fires are put out in stages. A fire is considered "contained" when it is surrounded by a line of suppression measures that make it harder for the fire to spread, although it continues to burn actively within the line's bounds. A fire is considered "controlled" when a line of control has been so strengthened and secured that it is unlikely for the fire to escape its bounds. Before this point, firefighters will have cooled any hotspots adjacent to the line and removed unburnt fuel in the surrounding area. Even in a "controlled" fire, the line of control can sometimes be disrupted—for instance, by a strong gust of wind—and if this happens, the fire can spread again.

In our school communities, many unexpected "hotspots" arose for school leaders as the pandemic raged on. Focused intently on ensuring safety for our school communities, we worked on containment. How can we safely get work to our students? How can we make sure they have food? How can we acquire and provide the technology that will assist learning at home? We weren't looking for other hotspots or sources of fuel that could flare up in the future; we just wanted to minimize the fire's immediate effects. But other hotspots, fanned by the pressures of the shutdown, ignited into wildfires of their own. In the wake of George Floyd's murder, unaddressed racial inequalities erupted into protests and intense debate over Critical Race Theory in our colleges and schools. Issues around vaccinations, masking, and social distancing became political hotspots. In later months, heat shifted to the debate over accommodations for transgender students and curricula that supports the LGBTQ community.

How have we worked to "contain" the chaos of our circumstances over the past two years? What does it mean to take "control" of our situation? Is that a desirable and attainable goal? And when so much seems out of our hands, how can we control the one thing we always have some power over: ourselves?

## Containing the Damage

When the pandemic first occurred, many of us waited anxiously for medical professionals to provide not just updates on the numbers of people infected, but some idea of how we would get a handle on this pandemic. Inconsistent information from people we traditionally look to as authorities—health care experts, political leaders—left us more confused and panicked than before. Leaders are supposed to do the right thing, but what was the right thing?

**BRENÉ BROWN ON CONTROL, STRESS, AND VULNERABILITY[1]**
Acclaimed author and motivational speaker Brené Brown offers informative insights about how our minds and bodies cope with stressful situations that feel out of our control:

> "We feel stressed when we evaluate environmental demand as beyond our ability to cope successfully. This includes elements of unpredictability, uncontrollability, and feeling overloaded."

> "Stressful situations cause both physiological (body) and psychological (mind and emotion) reactions. However, regardless of how strongly our body responds to stress (increase in heart rate and cortisol), our emotional reaction is more tied to our cognitive assessment of whether we can cope."

> "If stress is like being in the weeds, feeling overwhelmed is like being blown. Overwhelmed means an extreme level of stress, and emotional and/or cognitive intensity to the point of feeling unable to function."

> "Vulnerability is the emotion that we experience during times of uncertainty, risk, and emotional exposure . . . There is no courage without vulnerability. Courage requires the willingness to lean into uncertainty, risk, and emotional exposure."

> "In my most recent research on courage and leadership, the ability to embrace vulnerability emerged as the prerequisite for all the daring leadership behaviors. If we can't handle uncertainty, risk, and emotional exposure in a way that aligns with our values and furthers our organizational goals, we can't lead."

The result has been what author Joseph Myers calls "cultural vertigo"—a sense of profound disorientation in which "people lose their sense of who they are in the world."[2] Lacking clear leadership, people attempted to control their environment and sought security by affiliating with likeminded others. Some emphasized the necessity of public health measures for safety; others felt that safeguarding civil liberties was of higher importance. Each side could point to data and anecdotal evidence to back up their position.

When students from Pre-K through college were sent home abruptly, there was little time to think through all the implications. Classwork could be completed virtually, but it was more difficult to make up the missed social and athletic opportunities. Technology-based instruction delivered information to students but engaged them very little. Many teachers were forced to move to tasks that sacrificed rigor for grades. With the lack of consistency came feelings of lost control. Some districts went back and forth between live and virtual instruction as pandemic caseloads varied. Some placed the onus of the choice on students and their parents, creating a burden for teachers to deliver instruction in two different modes during the same semester, for in-person and online students. The lack of coordination has been disorienting for students, exhausting for teachers, and wasteful of district resources. It all seems . . . out of control.

## What is Control?

"Control" rarely has a positive connotation, unless we're referring to self-control. For many people it is a trigger word implying the loss of freedom. The thought of taking "control" can scare us, and that is okay. Enjoying control too much can definitely be a problem. Some leaders, perhaps out of a sense of insecurity, use control heavy-handedly to remind themselves and others that they are powerful. This type of control can produce compliance, but not engagement—a fact that's just as relevant in the faculty meeting as the classroom.

Despite some negative connotations, control is an important and even necessary characteristic in a leader. No one wants to be part of a chaotic institution. An extremely controlling leader and one who is so hands-off that chaos reigns are both harmful extremes. But a sweet spot near the center will allow a leader to lead in such a way that people have the confidence to follow.

> An extremely controlling leader and one who is so hands-off that chaos reigns are both harmful extremes. But a sweet spot near the center will allow a leader to lead in such a way that people have the confidence to follow.

## You Can't Put Out Every Fire

We've talked about containing fires and controlling fires. But what about putting out the fire altogether? Isn't that the ultimate goal? The fact of the matter is, sometimes containment and control are the best that can be achieved, at least for the foreseeable future. This is true both literally and metaphorically.

In the midst of the many disruptions to control we'll continue to experience throughout our lives, there is some good news: We can always exert self-control. A helpful way to think about this is to consider the possibility of primary control versus secondary control. When we achieve primary control, we take action to change a situation. When we can't do that, we can focus instead on secondary control: changing our attitude or orientation to a situation. This does not mean we accept or ignore social injustice or other deeply endemic social problems. Focusing on secondary control simply means evaluating and adjusting our own behavior— something we can always do, even as we work for enduring changes in an often chaotic world.

Compare this shift in thinking to the stages of grief we discussed earlier. It's not right that someone dear to us died and our future will forever be different than we wished it to be. Still, we find we can live our best life when we accept the reality of that loss and then figure out how to move on, finding joy and fulfillment in what we do have. Similarly, as we continue to move forward in the face of seemingly immovable issues, using our influence to get others to do the same, we can improve our effectiveness and resilience with a healthy sense of secondary control. We can remind ourselves that some problems are too big to solve alone, but that our efforts are still important as part of a long-term collective effort to build the society we want for ourselves and our descendants. We can avoid discouragement by looking to examples from the past, realizing how very far we've come on some issues, and how sudden leaps forward can happen when the right people are in the right place at the right time. We can also accept the reality that progress on thorny issues is often gradual; we will lose our influence and the patience of those we lead if we focus only on issues that have a long-term payoff. Therefore, we will continue to seek short-term and medium-term gains on other issues, building our relational capital and influence in ways that can move all these issues forward, even the most difficult ones.

## Building Self-Control and Self-Awareness

We can grow our own sense of self-control by learning about three of its subtypes: impulse control, emotional control, and movement control.[3]

Impulse control involves stopping to reflect before acting. We show impulse control when we think through the potential consequences of our actions. Emotional control refers to using our future goals to help us manage our feelings in the moment. We demonstrate emotional control when we practice delayed gratification, or continue toward a long-term goal despite setbacks and disappointments. Movement control means controlling the ways we use our body.[4]

Building self-awareness will help us develop our ability to control our thoughts, behaviors, and emotions in the face of difficulties. Self-awareness also helps us lead others well. A study of more than 1,000 leaders in more than 800 companies in more than 100 countries found that "leaders at the highest levels tend to have better self-awareness than leaders lower in the hierarchy."[5]

What are some ways we can build self-awareness and, with it, self-control? An article in *Harvard Business Review* on self-awareness in leaders offers several strategies:

- **Adopt a daily mindfulness practice.** To be mindful is to be fully present in the moment, sensing and feeling the current happenings without reaction or judgment. "Mindfulness training enables you to expand your awareness of what's happening in the landscape of your mind from moment to moment. It helps you to notice and regulate your emotions, and it helps you to better understand the behavior, reactions, and emotions of the people you lead—and in turn create better relations and lead for more impact."[6] Breathing exercises, doing one thing at a time (vs. multitasking), and noticing our sensations in the midst of everyday tasks are mindfulness exercises that increase our sense of self-awareness.

- **Take regular breaks.** Put down your phone, ignore the news for a bit, and spend a few minutes in quiet. "Taking regular short breaks, of even just one minute, gets you out of habitual thinking and behavior. It provides you space for awareness to arise and to see things clearer."[7]

- **Pay real attention to what others say.** "When we are busy, our brain defaults to pattern recognition. It wants simplicity. And when others talk to you, your brain will automatically look for what it has heard before and eliminate what is new....To avoid the brain's default pattern recognition, make an effort to listen with two ears wide open, and mouth shut, when you are with others....Be open. Be curious. And question your assumptions."

## Effectiveness, Efficiency, and Leading So Others Will Follow

As we continue to build our own self-awareness, how can we develop and implement other leadership traits that will result in others wanting to follow? We can learn from the example of two teachers, Amy and Jennifer.

Amy, a new fourth grade teacher, was eager to try "voice and choice"—a classroom technique she had just learned in professional development that would give children low-risk/high-success experiences to take charge of their own learning. After one attempt, she felt deflated. Most of the kids were enjoying it: some had chosen to play games, some were watching a movie, others were reading, doing art, or just talking to each other. One girl, however, just sat at her desk, frozen. Children with trauma and perfectionist tendencies are particularly likely to struggle when given a choice with no boundaries. Fearing reprisal or rejection, they can become overwhelmed by an anxiety of choosing the wrong thing. But the activity was aimless for the rest of the kids as well: Without developmentally appropriate scaffolding, the students had unclear expectations and did not acquire transferable skills that would produce growth.

Amy had wonderful intentions and enthusiasm, but she was not exercising control in a way that would have placed boundaries around the activity to make it effective for the whole class. The freedom was so vast that her students couldn't follow where she intended to lead. Had she put in place a choice boundary limiting the number of options, overwhelmed students might have felt less uncertain of how to proceed. Additional boundaries could have made the new activity more beneficial for the rest of the students and led to more meaningful and enthusiastic engagement.

Jennifer had come to me as a highly recommended teacher. After a few weeks, though, some of her grade-level coworkers hinted to me that they thought she wasn't a very hard worker. She didn't stay as long after the contract day ended as they did, and she never seemed to take home stacks of papers to grade. Every time they passed her room it looked like students were just up and socializing, instead of sitting and doing their work.

When I checked in on Jennifer's class, I found the students avidly engaged in active learning, moving around, and working on learning targets actively facilitated by their teacher. In a conversation with her later that day, I commended her for her mastery of active learning techniques and asked about her planning process. Every teacher had an hour and a half of planning time during the school day. Jennifer used hers efficiently, and assigned grades to students based on formative and summative assessments rather than sending home daily worksheets. From the outside looking in, sometimes the class looked chaotic. In reality, Jennifer was focused on the end goal of being an effective teacher, and through her active learning approach she was exerting control in a way that was highly effective for her students' learning. Despite her coworkers' concerns, I found that her methods met best practices and her planning process was a model of efficiency that promised to prevent early burnout.

## Freedom in the Framework

Kathryn was a school leader concerned about one of her English teachers, who had spent a full nine weeks working through *Romeo and Juliet*. Kathryn wanted to respect the teacher's freedom to choose how to teach necessary skills, but at the same time had a responsibility to make sure instruction met appropriate standards for the needs and requirements of the students. The teacher's process was to spend three weeks with students reading the text with partners in class, followed by another week of watching the play in movie form. This met a standard in her grade level that required comparing and contrasting a book and movie, but the investment of class time was excessive.

Kathryn handled the situation well. Instead of taking what might have seemed like the most direct and efficient approach by forcing the teacher to change, she waited for the teacher to take part in an English department exercise of mapping the skills and standards the students needed to know. At the end of the exercise, this teacher and her peers realized that many of the high priority skills and standards on their list were not being addressed by the current curriculum.

It was an "aha" moment. Once the teacher was aware of the priorities and framework, she made her own decision to spend less time on in-class reading and to show clips of the *Romeo and Juliet* movie rather than the entire film. One day during instruction a student mentioned that the plotline of *Romeo and Juliet* was similar to that of the 2021 remake of *West Side Story*. The entire class perked up, and the teacher seized on the idea of giving students the opportunity to choose from a plethora of books and movies based on the play to increase their comprehension and engagement. The end result was more effective, and more enjoyable for both the teacher and the students. Rather than take an authoritarian approach and implement changes from the top down, Kathryn, the administrator, exercised control by looking toward the most effective end result and establishing a training framework to influence her teachers.

## Empowering Students through "Accelerating Engagement"

As Kathryn's example shows, sometimes we hold onto control more effectively by stepping back and granting agency to others, influencing—not dictating—the direction they choose to go. This applies not only in administrative situations, but in how we teach. In any given situation, we need to ask ourselves whether it would be more productive to step back or step in, and whether the most direct or "efficient" approach is actually the most effective way to move forward.

> Sometimes we hold onto control more effectively by stepping back and granting agency to others, while influencing—not dictating—the direction they choose to go.

Accelerating Engagement—a model developed by Meteor Education through research into psychology, change management, and education—is a useful program for making a transition from a more traditional top-down approach to one that is more learner-driven.

Many new programs function like "spinning tops"—they start out with great energy, then lose momentum as other needs demand attention and leaders and their advocates leave. Accelerating Engagement should be envisioned more like a flywheel. As we start turning the wheel, progress is slow and incremental, and resistance may be strong. But as more hands work together and successively add energy to the spin, it begins to move faster, more easily, and with greater energy. Let's look a little more closely at the three major components of engagement represented in this flywheel: Relational, Cognitive, and Agentic.

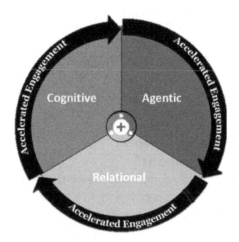

*Meteor Education's Accelerating Engagement flywheel*

Everything begins with relational engagement. In this model, relational engagement can take place learner-to-peer, learner-to-leader (or instructor), learner-to-future self, and learner-to-content areas. We all come to relationships differently based on our experiences, personality traits, and developmental levels. Regardless of our different starting points, we all benefit when we sense trust is building, when we feel supported, when we're challenged to learn, and when we know we are accepted at school or work. Healthy relational interaction is a differentiator between compliance and engagement. As we move out of the pandemic, building or rebuilding our relationships is an essential first step toward regaining control in our classrooms, schools, and communities.

Cognitive engagement can mean tackling tasks with purposiveness, energy, and strategy; making an intentional investment in learning; and engaging in metacognition and self-regulated learning. Basically, cognitive engagement refers to the extent to which students are willing and able to take on the learning task at hand even when it becomes difficult. We may need to scaffold some skills, but students have the cognitive ability to take on the task. Cognitive engagement may require building skills to ensure that learners are prepared for the task ahead, but we should not fall into the trap of getting stuck at the cognitive level. The level of rigor and skills needed for the task will dictate the time spent in cognitive engagement.

Agentic engagement is the learners' constructive contribution to the flow of instruction they receive as they express their interests and offer their input. Agentic engagement is a purposive, proactive, and reciprocal type of engagement. Its essential purpose is to recruit greater autonomy as well as support from the leader or instructor. Agency is a crucial component of engaged learning. Even with adult learners, we may need to intentionally support and thoughtfully encourage agentic engagement until trust is built. The concept is relatively new (most research began in 2010) and efficacy trials are ongoing. Many educators have heard of agentic engagement, but few have been trained in it or its practices. What we know is that the more agentic engagement learners experience, the greater longitudinal gains they report in perceived autonomy-supportive teaching, such as greater perspective-taking and personally relevant learning activities.

This flywheel may start moving slowly as trust is built and students and instructors become accustomed to a more student-centered way of learning. Following the pandemic, the relational engagement between students and teachers as well as among students will go a long way toward building momentum. As the flywheel continues to rotate, the relational, cognitive, and agentic engagement will deepen. Potential for growth and support will be present with each spin, and new needs requiring scaffolding may come to light. The goal of the flywheel is for the learner to generate their own energy as they continue their process of learning.

We sometimes have a tendency to want to invest extra time in our "rock stars": the staff or students who consistently overperform and need additional challenges. These individuals, however, are highly self-motivated, and can be set free within a framework to devise for themselves new and more clever ways of accomplishing their work, whether that be teaching or learning. Giving them agency in this way can free up the leader's or instructor's resources to focus on those who need a little extra feedback, encouragement, or gentle prodding to push themselves. The time required to implement the flywheel will start relatively high at the beginning, and will greatly decrease as engagement is accelerated for all members of the group.

## What We Can Always Control

In education, we'll be able to extinguish some of the "fires" we encounter, while others will require an intense, enduring response that still doesn't quite achieve the results we want. In our ideal educational system, the "fires" wouldn't ever ignite; everything would run smoothly, no one would get hurt, and there would be no danger of a catastrophic breakdown. But that's not a realistic goal for any of our social institutions, educational or otherwise. We will always have problems to deal with. Some problems will be unearthed that are so deeply buried, that are so endemic, that our best efforts to influence them will not make a dent. What do we do in that case?

We keep moving forward.

Systemic issues such as racism, violence, inequality, gender discrimination, and necessary reforms in our education, healthcare, and other institutions are too important to give up on, just because they are difficult and we can't pull out quick satisfying wins. As former U.S. Senator Paul Wellstone famously said, "If we don't fight hard enough for the things we stand for, at some point we have to recognize that we don't really stand for them." Yes, we go for the low-hanging fruit first, to win the trust of those who look to our leadership, to help them begin to follow and emulate, and to use their own influence to get things turning. But we don't camp out under the low-hanging fruit. We draw upon our growing relational capital and influence to take on difficult challenges, even if a full resolution proves to be a multigenerational effort.

> We draw upon our growing relational capital and influence to take on difficult challenges, even if a full resolution proves to be a multigenerational effort.

Disrupted control drains us of power and increases the impact of a traumatic event. When we've lost some control we might respond by jealously guarding what we still have, resisting beneficial change. Sharing control can allow a school community to rebuild relational engagement. Engaged teachers, students, leaders, and school community members will together create an unstoppable force to face the difficulties ahead and ignite innovation.

And as we inevitably encounter challenges that seem insurmountable and crises we cannot avoid, we can continue to lean on the truth that when all is in upheaval, we do still have power—the power to reflect upon and influence our own emotions, our own reactions, and our own thoughtful next steps. We cannot control what each day brings, but we can control how we respond to it.

## REFLECTION QUESTIONS

1. How have you and your team experienced "cultural vertigo"? How has this altered your outlook on life?

2. If the focus of your thinking were to shift from "control" to "influence," what new opportunities would that open for you to effect positive change in your institution?

3. What ideas were sparked for you in the discussion of establishing frameworks within which people may exercise choice? Who would need to cooperate in implementing this idea?

4. How can you grow your own self-awareness? How could becoming more self-aware help you to lead others well?

### STRAIGHTFORWARD SURVIVAL

When we experience disruption, sometimes we need simple ideas for taking a next, practical step forward. If you are unsure of where to start, choose one of these ideas from the chapter:

- Focus on building positive relationships. Who can you connect with this week, either in person, on the phone, or through a text or email?

- Reflect on what you can control and influence.

- Seek solutions to short-term and medium-term issues, not just long-term ones. What's something you can resolve today?

## ENDNOTES

1.  B. Brown, (2022), *Atlas of the Heart: Mapping Meaningful Connection and the Language of Human Experience.* Random House, Inc. 5-6, 13-14.

2.  J. Myers, (2022, April 4). Personal communication.

3.  M. Brunetti, (n.d.). "Here's How to Help Kids Master the 3 types of self-control," *The Instillery.* Retrieved April 18, 2022, from https://www.the-instillery. com/story/heres-how-to-help-kids-master-the-3-types-of-self-control.

4.  Ibid.

5.  R. Hougaard, (2018, March 7). "Self-awareness can help leaders more than an MBA can." *Harvard Business Review.* Retrieved April 18, 2022, from https://hbr. org/2018/01/self-awareness-can-help-leaders-more-than-an-mba-can.

6.  Ibid.

7.  Ibid.

# CHAPTER 7: RESTORING COMMUNICATION
## Listening and Speaking in a Storm

Steve was 11 years old in 2008 when Hurricane Ike passed over his home in a Houston apartment complex. As he remembers,

It started getting windy around 6 p.m. (winds around 40 mph) and we got scared and ran home. Twigs and leaves were flying everywhere. I couldn't stand against the wind, it kept pushing me back. That night the wind was howling constantly. A strong gust made the carport downstairs start rumbling. My mom was terrified and we tried to calm her down. Around 12:30 a.m. we lost power and the wind got louder. It sounded like a train one minute and a wolf howling the next. We opened the door to get a peek. It was terrifying! In a sea of darkness the palm trees were bending back and forth violently, water was pouring from the roofs like Niagara Falls, the giant pine trees were bending at 45-degree angles and branches were snapping off. An hour later, the back window shattered and rain started to pour in. We covered the TV and computer with trash bags to protect them. Around 2 a.m. the winds reached over 75 mph and we heard debris hitting the building. All night the wind was screaming. We spent probably 12 hours in the closet until noon Saturday. We were scared out of our wits and I cried but my mom reassured me that we made it and we are OK. I was thankful that we didn't lose our home or our lives, for that matter.[1]

## SURVIVING THE STORM

People weathering a hurricane are full of adrenaline and on high alert. It isn't a time to be polite or tiptoe around each other's feelings. We feel the screaming winds and crashing debris, and existential fear pares down our communication to survival basics. No long-range planning here, no smoothing out the wrinkles of past relationship problems—just the minimum necessary to get through the night alive. Our survival response to catastrophic conditions is trauma, a combination of emotional numbness and hypervigilance. Once events stabilize and a sense of normalcy returns, most people can frame the experience as an event and move forward. For some, however, their trauma remains a daily battle to avoid situations that trigger an extreme fight or flight response. As we step into our roles as leaders through times of trauma, we need to understand how trauma brings about disruptions in communication and how we can respond to those disruptions in a way that helps us move into post-traumatic growth.

## Trauma and the Brain

Quite simply, trauma changes how the brain works. As in the example of Hurricane Ike and its impact on Steve and his family, trauma survivors simplify their communication to the basics needed to survive a traumatic event. During a crisis, the amygdala—the part of the brain that manages survival instincts—becomes activated and draws energy away from areas of the brain that store memories and engage in higher-order reasoning.

Ongoing stress reshapes our brains. Prolonged stress "may adversely affect the prefrontal lobe (responsible for language), causing problems with communication. It can also shrink the hippocampus (responsible for memory), leading to poor memory and concentration."[2] Dr. Kerry Ressler, a professor of psychiatry at Harvard Medical School, says that studies of animals that have endured prolonged periods of stress show that those animals "have less activity in the parts of their brain that handle higher-order tasks—for example, the prefrontal cortex—and more activity in the primitive parts of the brain that are focused on survival, such as the amygdala."[3] When the brain is under continuous stress, "it essentially builds up the parts of the brain designed to handle threats, and the part of the brain tasked with more complex thought takes a backseat."[4]

## COVID BRAIN

Emerging research continues to show that COVID can damage the brain. The following are seven ways COVID can negatively impact the brain:

1. **Brain shrinkage.** In a British study of MRI scans taken before and after COVID, "one of the biggest surprises to researchers was a decrease in brain volume. Compared to those who weren't infected, the COVID group had 0.2% to 2% more shrinkage."

2. **Up to a decade of brain aging.** "According to UK researchers, a 2% reduction in brain volume is roughly equivalent to 10 years of aging."

3. **The cerebellum takes a hit.** Some of the brain shrinkage noted in COVID patients resulted from the loss of volume in the cerebellum, which is involved in coordinating thought and motor processes. "It is essential for processing complex information and is involved in processing speed. When the cerebellum is low in activity, people are more likely to be clumsy and to have difficulty solving complex problems. They process their thoughts more slowly and tend to get confused more often than those with healthy cerebellum activity."

4. **Thinning in certain brain regions.** This thinning was noted in the orbitofrontal cortex and parahippocampal gyrus. The thinning in the orbitofrontal cortex is related to the common COVID symptom of anosmia, the loss of one's sense of smell.

5. **Even mild COVID cases cause brain changes.** Though only 15 out of 401 participants in the British brain study were hospitalized from COVID, a much higher number of those 401 were at risk of harmful effects on the brain.

6. **Bigger impact in older adults.** Though participants in the study included those from a range of ages, the negative brain results "were more pronounced in the elderly."

7. **Overactivity in the brain's emotional centers.** "At Amen Clinics, before-and-after COVID brain SPECT scans show heightened activity in the limbic system, which is the brain's emotional center. Too much activity here is linked to an increased risk for depression and negativity."[5]

Because of all of this, our brains post-trauma are different from before. You've likely seen this in yourself. Maybe, years after the COVID pandemic first interrupted our lives, you still struggle occasionally to complete formerly routine tasks, like leading a meeting, composing an email, or remembering what's on your schedule for the day. This is typical and expected of a brain that has undergone long-term strain. Someone who has been through trauma may exhibit trouble focusing or concentrating on a task at hand, have difficulty expressing emotions, show reluctance to trust others, or have a problem asking for or receiving help. They may appear withdrawn or disengaged or lash out against those they spend time with.[6]

School leaders need to recognize that communication is greatly impacted and impaired by trauma. Acknowledging the existence of the "trauma brain" and its limitations will allow us to help our communities move forward.

## Providing Space that Accommodates the Processing of Trauma

Leaders in school settings must respond compassionately and effectively to those who have been through trauma and loss. Some key points to remember as you move forward:

1. **Make it clear that you are available.** Whether you're working with a staff member, a student, a parent, or an entire community that has been through trauma, you must show that you are available as a resource, to listen, to talk, and to provide help coping. Reach out to the traumatized person or persons. Let them know when and how you are available and who else on the team (for instance, a school counselor) is also ready to serve as a resource, support, and listening ear. Share this information more than once, remembering that the trauma brain has difficulty retaining information and is overcoming many emotions that get in the way of what might ordinarily be a direct or timely response.

2. **Don't take it personally.** Irritability, lack of focus, anger, frustration, and fear are normal emotions in someone who has been through an intensely stressful situation. They may lash out, and you should be prepared for this to sometimes occur. Remember that this is not about you but is a symptom of how the other person's mind and body are responding to what has happened. Continue to provide space and maintain a calm presence even as you encounter negative or difficult emotions.

3. **Allow them to talk.** Don't come into a conversation with an agenda. Listen, ask open-ended questions, and avoid judgment, interruptions, or trying to fix things.[7] Understand that they might want to repeatedly share the same topics or memories as they process what they've been through.

## Recognizing Our Own Trauma

Remember the story from earlier in the book about 26-year veteran public educator Janet, whose confidence was repeatedly shaken during the pandemic? Criticism had come in unrelentingly from all sides. Faced with the overwhelming pressure of meeting students' basic needs, fielding and responding to public backlash about mask policies and other hot-button topics, and being personally sued, Janet's confidence was shaken. Her ability to communicate effectively plummeted. As educators, we can likely relate to aspects of Janet's story. As we make every effort to apply best practices and enact well-researched communication strategies, we need to remember that our ability to communicate has been damaged. We are as susceptible to trauma brain as those we are tasked and called to lead.

After any trauma, we must look after our mental and physical health and prioritize our well-being. We may need to ensure we get adequate sleep, spend time with friends and family, and use time off when we need it.

## Rebuilding Trust to Communicate Effectively

When you don't fully trust yourself or others, it can feel impossible to communicate effectively. Others may hesitate to believe what you're saying, or they may struggle to understand and apply what is intended because of their trauma brain. To redevelop trust, we must first lower distrust. The five following suggestions are actions that lower distrust and develop the ability to decide to trust.

1. **Express your commitment to the relationship.** Let those who've been through trauma know that you are available for support over the long haul.
2. **Create routines.** Work to reimplement a structured, predictable pattern to your days to restore a sense of stability.
3. **Speak about the future** and make plans to remind those who have been through trauma of what the future can hold.
4. **Keep your promises.** Do what you say you're going to do. Show up when you say you will. Your consistency and reliability will help to foster trust.

5. **Look for ways to empower others.** As time passes, give those who have been through trauma more choices and control to help build their self-confidence.[8]

## Three Goals of Crisis Communication

We must continually work to rebuild trust. As we do so, we should also consider the role of a leader's communication. During a crisis, communication from leadership should reduce stress, provide verifiable information, and communicate in a human voice. Let's consider some practical, actionable steps in each area to help restore disrupted communication.

### 1. REDUCE STRESS

Workplace stress is a problem across all industries. In the United States, an estimated 36% of workers struggle with work-related stress that costs $30 billion annually in lost workdays. Stress contributes to workplace accidents that cost an estimated $50 billion in 2014.[9] Employers are becoming increasingly aware of a responsibility to provide for physical healthcare needs and facilitate mental health and wellness.

### REDUCING WORKPLACE STRESS

Alan Kohll at *Forbes* has compiled several valuable suggestions to reduce workplace stress, some of which could be implemented by individuals and others that require coordination by the employer. A few of these that are most translatable to an academic setting are:

- **Walking groups:** Exercise and community reduce stress. Faculty might decide to use their lunch break or take some time before or after school to walk and decompress.

- **Switch to decaf:** Caffeine helps us get going in the morning. It also intensifies stress and has a half-life of about three to five hours. Switching to decaffeinated coffee around noon reduces caffeine intake by 97%.

- **Open door policy:** Many people are stressed because of confusion about what leadership or colleagues are doing. Employees should be encouraged to approach the leadership with their questions without fear of rebuke or reprisals.

- **Positive messaging:** The words we use can help create an encouraging workplace culture. Choose personal, encouraging, passionate, and empowering words in your messages to individuals and the organization.

- **Clear communication:** When leadership sends ambiguous, inconsistent, or confusing messages, they significantly raise employee stress. To reduce stress, define expectations clearly, offer encouragement, and actively solicit questions.

- **Healthy snacking:** Snacking on greasy or carb-heavy foods provides a quick burst of energy followed by a crash and burn. Provide healthy snacks for employees at work or educate them about the snacks that offer long-lasting energy for a demanding day.

- **Inspirational quotes:** Consider positive quotes as part of an email signature, in weekly newsletters, or posted on bulletin boards and bathroom stalls. Tie positive quotes to current events or situations or choose quotes to build on a theme to avoid the quotes coming across as trite or random.

- **Meaningful meetings:** Busy employees feel stressed by pointless meetings that take them away from more critical tasks or stress-relieving activities. Consider using email to replace meetings that simply pass along information or check on status updates. If meeting in person is part of a strategy to keep employees connected, design activities and discussions to accomplish that goal.

- **Clear expectations:** Some employees, particularly newer ones, may stress about what is expected of them. They know their duties but may not understand how those duties fit into the bigger picture and exactly how to accomplish them. They need to understand what is and is not their responsibility.

- **Sincere compliments:** A heartfelt compliment is golden in an environment where people feel a barrage of criticism from every side. When the source of stress cannot be removed but must be endured as part of the job, a compliment can make the burden lighter and get a more positive train of thought going.

- **Don't micromanage:** Steve Jobs said, "It doesn't make sense to hire smart people and tell them what to do; we hire smart people so they can tell us what to do." Let people do their jobs and get involved only when necessary or helpful to do so. [10]

## SURVIVING THE STORM

## NAVIGATING THE CHALLENGES OF INTERPERSONAL COMMUNICATION

Interpersonal communication in times of stress is a tough challenge, especially when we encounter disagreement, criticism, or conflict. Under stress and duress, our amygdalas scan for danger rather than listen to the other person with an open mind.

Criticism can feel personal and hurtful. When you are on the receiving end, respond by restating what the person said to make sure you heard it accurately. If necessary, tell them you will think about it and talk to them later.

Before responding, ask yourself a few questions:

*Is it true? How do I know?*

*Could the opposite be true?*

*Can I do anything about it?*

*Do I want to do anything about it?*

*Do I see a pattern in my communication?*

*Could I be miscommunicating?*

During a heated conversation, our instincts jump to conclusions. When our amygdalas kick in, our minds don't slow down to examine the facts. It happens so often there is an acronym to describe it: NIMSU—or No Information, Make Stuff Up.

## THE "BE CALM" STRATEGY

Try this 6-point strategy for managing challenging comments from others "in the moment."

**B – Breathe:** Take a few deep, calming breaths before responding. Do not respond until you are ready.

**E – Evaluate:** Is this a jab that can be ignored, or is it a true conflict that must be addressed?

**C – Care:** Proceed with care. Is your perception accurate? How are others reacting? Read the room.

**A – Address:** If the comment must be addressed, set up a time to meet, perhaps with a third party.

**L – Leave:** Excuse yourself from the situation as soon as possible and get away to give yourself time to calm down.

**M – Meditate:** Remind yourself of your competence, goodness, and worth. Refuse to let this situation define you.

In his book *Crucial Conversations: Tools for Talking When Stakes are High*, Joseph Grenny offers many valuable insights that apply to the kinds of tense conversations we can find ourselves in every day, especially during times of crisis. His tips include:

- **Start with the heart.** Consider what you want and what's at stake.

- **Learn to look.** If you or the other person is becoming defensive, say, "I think we've moved away from dialogue," and get back on track.

- **Make it safe.** Diminish defensiveness by apologizing, seeking others' views, and taking time outs.

- **Master your story.** Focus on what happened to cause you to feel as you do. Think through your emotions and choose the best response.

- **Revisit your path.** Share your story and perceptions so the other person can see where you are coming from.

- **Explore the other person's path.** Find out what they are thinking, and make sure you understand and look for areas of agreement.

- **Move to action.** Find agreement, document who will do what, by when, by what path, and decide how and when you will report your progress. [11]

Finally, if there is nothing we can do to change the contentious narrative, we need to decide how to implement healthy boundaries. Is it necessary to stay in contact with this person because of family or professional obligations? Then we can choose to maintain a professional demeanor, not to speak negatively about the person to others, and maintain appropriate boundaries. If the relationship is not essential, we can exclude them from our lives and move on. Doing this is a gift to ourselves, not a concession to the other person.

---

### THE FOUR HORSEMEN OF THE APOCALYPSE

Dr. John Gottman is well known for his research on marital conflicts. After studying thousands of couples, he concluded that four toxic behaviors are the most damaging to a relationship. Those toxic behaviors indicate a high probability of divorce. These "Four Horsemen of the Apocalypse" are criticism, contempt, defensiveness, and stonewalling (refusing to talk). We need to be on the lookout and learn to identify these "horsemen" to remove them from our repertoire.

Gottman suggests watching for and using "repair attempts" to cool down a heated discussion. A repair attempt can be an affirming statement, a light touch on the hand or arm if appropriate, or an effort at humor. When we attempt to repair, we signal that the other person and the relationship are important to us. When we notice our conversation partner using repair strategies, we need to acknowledge that, reciprocate, and turn down the heat.[12]

---

### 2. PROVIDE VERIFIABLE INFORMATION

Social media contributed to two problems: information overload and cognitive bias. This combination caused incredible damage, eroding confidence in leaders and institutions and creating civil unrest. Social media produced an overload of sketchy information, with rumors and conjecture drowning out credible sources of facts and science. The virus was new, experts were learning, and topics like R numbers that determine the rate of the spread of a virus and lethality were too nuanced and complex for the public to understand. Together, all of this led to a perfect storm of confusion and conflict.

## FROM CABIN FEVER TO RIOTS

A forest fire needs three things—dry conditions, a spark, and continuing fuel. That's why George Floyd's killing rapidly flared to global protests and waves of violence. The stress of the worldwide quarantine provided the tinderbox conditions. Social media fanned the flames as the videos | of Floyd's helpless pleas and the behavior of the officers went viral.

At an individual level, people are responsible for their own decisions about whom and what they will trust, but as leaders of institutions responsible for the knowledge, health, and wellbeing of thousands of children, it is incumbent upon us to make sure the information we disseminate is well-vetted. Employees may circulate rumors, speculate about causes, or imply threats. Don't try to respond to the specifics in a story, but do acknowledge the concern behind statements or questions. Develop a disciplined response that might include statements like:

- "This is what we know."
- "This is what we are looking into."
- "Here are some sources that you might find helpful in answering your questions."
- "Please share your questions and concerns, and we will work to find answers."
- "Circumstances will often change until things stabilize, and we will regularly share what we know and what we are learning."

In *The Elements of Journalism*, Bill Kovach and Tom Rosenstiel include the discipline of verification as one of the standards of responsible reporting. Because journalists must make decisions about what to report and how to report it, they are not objective, but they use objective methods to gather factual information. These include consulting multiple witnesses, disclosing their sources as much as possible, and asking for comment from more than one side.[13]

These practices are valuable not just to journalists, but to all of us. If the media always reflects someone's bias—and it does—then how can we find verifiable information? Two ways: by choosing sources that report facts and fact-based analysis, and by being aware of the partisan leanings of news sources and listening to each side's interpretations of the facts. Ad Fontes Media has analyzed the biases of various media sources in The Media Bias Chart.[14] This is a highly useful tool for classroom discussions and projects related to media bias, and may also be beneficial to staff and parents in making the most informed decisions about their media choices.

A district, school, or individual teacher has to consider not only high-level national or international news that impacts us and our students, but how to gather accurate information about the micro-level events that can lead to institutional improvement, conflict resolution, or disciplinary action.

Even when eyewitnesses are present, their testimony may not be accurate—or at least not immediately so. Joseph Myers points out that a hyper-focused trauma brain doesn't immediately account for everything that is going on around the person experiencing the trauma. They may have absorbed information following a traumatic event, but it takes time for the brain to process what's taken place. In fact, the brain may not remember everything that happened until the person has gone through at least two sleep cycles. As a result, someone interviewed immediately after a trauma may not be able to remember all the details and may construct false memories, making it appear as if they are lying or have changed their story. Moreover, it is easy to start a rumor right after an event that is not accurate because the whole story has not yet been remembered and told. People need time and space to remember the story, and grace for the fact that their initial impressions may not be accurate.[15]

Our communities need to understand that media bias and inaccuracies in eyewitness accounts are nothing new. What is new is that the current level of technology has given global exposure to even the most obscure viewpoints, making it difficult to distinguish between factual, journalistically rigorous data and analysis versus opinion drawn from unreliable sources, rumors, or imagination. As educators, we can see this as an opportunity to equip our students and the community with the tools they need to apply critical thinking skills to their chosen sources of information.

### 3. COMMUNICATE IN A HUMAN VOICE
We can deliver incredibly clear, precise communication and still come across as lacking in humanity. In times of crisis and difficulty, people expect leaders not only to provide information, but a sense of reassurance and safety. These vulnerable communications are opportunities to develop and deepen relationships with people we work, study, and socialize with.

In even the most mundane communications, we want to make sure we are building understanding and strengthening the relationship between the communicator, the recipient, and, ultimately, the whole school community.

Empathetic communication requires the emotional intelligence to know when to listen with the *head* and when to listen with the *heart*—to understand not only *what* someone is saying but to empathize with them enough to envision *why* they might be saying it. Authentic conversation is an art that can't be scripted. It ebbs and flows depending upon the needs of the participants and the purpose of the conversation.

> Empathetic communication requires the emotional intelligence to know when to listen with the *head* and when to listen with the *heart.*

Good old-fashioned tact is a skill in short supply. We can see this in the example of Dr. Subczek, who worked for years as an associate professor before finally receiving a long-awaited promotion to full professor. Her joy was spoiled when in a meeting the dean shared that one member of the promotion committee had misgivings about her, which traced back to a past conflict between them. The dean's lack of tact led directly to Subczek's ill feelings. If the dean thought there was an issue she needed to work on, it would have been better to approach the topic in a different time and place, over a cup of coffee or during her annual performance review. Instead, his poorly-timed remarks in an unwelcome setting left her feeling deflated, angry at her colleague, and suspicious that the dean himself did not think she deserved the promotion.

There are instances when we must communicate primarily with either the head or the heart. In times of crisis, what we might think of as "brutally honest optimism" provides necessary balance and stability to a school community. This communication approach brings together both head and heart. Brutal honesty without optimism can seem harsh and create panic, despair, and resistance to leaders who may appear callous to the suffering of the community. On the other hand, over-optimism makes us appear cluelessly out of touch with reality and causes those under our leadership to look elsewhere for analysis and guidance. Put them together, though,

135

and brutally honest optimism validates the genuinely traumatic nature of a situation while still providing hope that motivates us to act, even with the full awareness that the journey ahead may not be easy.

Tact is not a skill that we all have in equal measure. Leaders who are lacking in it can leverage the skills of their teammates to make up for our own deficits. Good communication matters at every level, particularly under stressful circumstances. Teachers and staff are powerful conduits of information to the school community, and when they are unaware or unclear on school policies, misunderstandings will ensue. A case in point: A school district trying to pass a bond issue relayed information on the topic to the whole community before engaging staff members. Staff pushed back, feeling their concerns had been ignored, and as a result did not support the initiative in the community. As a result, the initiative failed at the ballot box. It was a full decade later before the school had the opportunity to try again. This time, the district took a different and more tactful course. They started with staff input, secured key stakeholders in the community, hosted collaborative work sessions, and had a strategic communication plan—resulting in a successful bond issue.

One of the main ways we can humanize our communication is to listen not only to what is said, but what is implied. One of my primary school teachers was fond of saying, "You have two ears and one mouth. That is because you need to listen twice as much as you talk." The statement was annoying and patronizing, but true nonetheless. Usually people don't listen to understand, they listen to respond. Power and Ego in Everyday Life, Charles Derber explains that in the United States a lack of social support prompts people to compete for attention and use various strategies to turn the course of a conversation toward themselves. People who are considered caring and talented conversationalists are those who cooperate in keeping the topic focused on the other person, rather than themselves.[16] Finally, consider what author Tim Keller wrote about healthy conversation: "Do all the work necessary until you can articulate the views of your opponent with such strength and clarity that he or she could say, 'I couldn't have said it better myself.'"[17]

## Restorative Communication

When communication has been disrupted, it must not only be restored, but restorative. What's the difference? Two parties who have not talked to one another for years might restore communication by picking up the phone, but if they immediately get into a yelling match, their communication is not *restorative*. Restorative communication heals a relationship, sometimes simply back to the pre-rupture state, but ideally leaving it even better and stronger than it ever was before.

Take Grace, a 16-year-old who said her relationship with her mother improved dramatically after a memorable fight. Emotions were running high on both sides and neither felt like the other was really listening. Finally, Grace screamed in frustration, "Don't you understand I'm not mad, I'm sad?!" Both Grace and her mother were shocked by this moment of truth; in fact, Grace said she had never really understood this about herself until that very instant. "I didn't like how she expressed it, but the truth of it hit me hard, because it's exactly like me," her mother said. "I realized she put into words what I had felt at her age, and something I had tried to get my husband to understand about me. It didn't even occur to me that I was misunderstanding Grace the same way I've felt misunderstood my whole life." After that pivotal night, Grace's mom feels more connected to her daughter and tries to listen not only to the words she speaks, but to consider what might be behind those words. For her part, Grace feels much freer to articulate her feelings, trusting they will be heard without her having to resort to emotional outbursts. And Grace's dad? Let's be honest: He's still trying to figure out what happened!

In the midst of a tense exchange, Grace and her mother found a moment of shared healing and humanity. They realized that they were more alike than they were different, and that realization helped them achieve a greater level of empathy. They stopped seeing one another as enemies, but as fellow well-meaning human beings with valid concerns that needed to be heard and addressed. Their communication was not only restored, but it was restorative, bringing their relationship to a better place than it had been before.

What can restorative communication look like in the classroom? Vynesha Johnson describes an all-too-familiar scenario in which a teacher was frustrated with one of his students, who was refusing to follow directions.[18] With some coaching, the teacher decided rather than treating it as a disciplinary issue to take a "restorative conversation approach." Johnson elaborates:

> Restorative conversations allow the teacher to demonstrate empathy, teach children how to resolve conflict, and most importantly, allow students to have a voice. It's an opportunity

for both the teacher and student to express their feelings about what's going on in the classroom while setting high expectations. When we do so, we actually humanize ourselves in the eyes of students. They begin to see us beyond the "teacher standing in front of them."[19]

Restorative conversations don't need to be elaborate; in fact, they can take place over just minutes in any situation in which teachers and students butt heads. The important elements of restorative conversations are to make the student feel cared about; to give voice to the student to tell their side; to communicate to the student how you felt about the situation; to reiterate high expectations; and to create a plan together for future success in meeting expectations. The results can be transformative. In Johnson's example, after this more conversational approach, the teacher better understood what was happening in the student's life and felt motivated to form more of a relationship with him. Sensing transparency and empathy, the student began to respond more cooperatively and even started urging other students to follow classroom expectations.[20]

Samantha White offers useful prompts for a successful restorative conversation.[21] When challenging someone's behavior as part of a meaningful and even healing conversation, we can ask:

1. What happened?
2. What were you thinking at the time?
3. What have you thought about since?
4. Who has been affected by what you did?
5. How have they been affected?
6. What do you think you need to do to make things right?

Restorative conversations may also be necessary with others who observed the behavior without directly taking part in it. To help those who have been affected, we can ask:

1. What did you think when you realized what had happened?
2. What impact has this incident had on you and others?
3. What has been the hardest thing for you about it?
4. What do you think needs to happen to make things right?

When it comes to complex problems, we obviously can't expect one brief conversation to fix everything and tie it up with a bow, but restorative conversation practices will help us keep moving in the right direction. We are not stuck where we are. We can apply a lesson here from what we know about our minds. Our brains have neuroplasticity—meaning the ability to change and adapt. When we put them in a healing environment, they can improve.[22] In a similar way, when we use restorative communication practices, we are working toward the goal of healed relationships.

## REFLECTION QUESTIONS

1. How have you seen examples of a "trauma brain" in yourself? In others?

2. What are some strategies you can employ the next time you are communicating with a person or team that has been through trauma?

3. What are ways that you can take care of yourself during periods of trauma or long-term stress? How do or could these practices help you?

4. Are you stronger in "head" or "heart" conversation? What do you imagine are some ways to develop your strengths in both areas?

5. What new possibilities might "brutally honest optimism" open up for you? How might it affect your relationships?

### STRAIGHTFORWARD SURVIVAL

When we experience disruption, sometimes we need simple ideas for taking a next, practical step forward. If you are unsure of where to start, choose one of these ideas from the chapter:

- Allow people to express themselves without judgment. Listen without thinking of what you'll say next.

- Provide opportunities in meetings for meaningful collaboration and communication. Who could you encourage more participation from?

- Give sincere, meaningful compliments to each school staff member. Set a reasonable timeframe to complete your first round.

## ENDNOTES

1. Adapted from: "Stories from Hurricane Survivors," (2021, February 3), National Weather Service. Retrieved February 18, 2022, from https://www.weather.gov/safety/hurricane-survivors.

2. R. Solon, "How Trauma-Informed Communication Improves Workplace Culture," (n.d.), *FEI Behavioral Health*. Retrieved April 6, 2022, from https://www.feinet.com/assets/uploads/2020/01/WPQ120_Trauma-Informed-Communication.pdf.

3. "Protect Your Brain from Stress," (2021, February 15), *Harvard Health*. Retrieved April 5, 2022, from https://www.health.harvard.edu/mind-and-mood/protect-your-brain-from-stress.

4. Ibid.

5. Warning: Before-and-After Covid Brain Scans Reveal Damage, (2022), Amen Clinics. Retrieved April 23, 2022, from https://www.amenclinics.com/blog/warning-before-and-after-covid-brain-scans-reveal-damage/.

6. How Trauma Can Affect Communication, (2021, January 28), Sana Counselling. Retrieved April 5, 2022, from https://sanacounselling.ca/blog/how-trauma-can-affect-communication.

7. R. Solon, How Trauma-Informed Communication Improves Workplace Culture, (n.d.), FEI Behavioral Health. Retrieved April 6, 2022, from https://www.feinet.com/assets/uploads/2020/01/WPQ120_Trauma-Informed-Communication.pdf.

8. Ibid.

9. C. Pazzanese, (2016, July 12), "The High Price of Workplace Stress," *Harvard Gazette*. Retrieved April 11, 2022, from https://news.harvard.edu/gazette/story/2016/07/the-high-price-of-workplace-stress/.

10. A. Kohll, (2021, December 10), "25 Ways to Cut Employee Stress and Boost Productivity," *Forbes*. Retrieved April 11, 2022, from https://www.forbes.com/sites/alankohll/2017/02/22/25-ways-to-cut-employee-stress-and-boost-productivity/.

11. J. Grenny, (2022), *Crucial Conversations: Tools for Talking When Stakes are High*, McGraw Hill.

12. J.M. Gottman and N. Silver, (2018), *The Seven Principles for Making Marriage Work: A Practical Guide from the International Bestselling Relationship Expert*. Orion Spring.

13. "The Elements of Journalism," (2021, July 15), *American Press Institute*. Retrieved April 11, 2022, from https://www.americanpressinstitute.org/journalism-essentials/what-is-journalism/elements-journalism/.

14. "Static Media Bias Chart." (2022, April 2), Ad Fontes Media. Retrieved April 11, 2022, from https://adfontesmedia.com/static-mbc/?utm_source=HomePage_.

15. J. Myers, (2022, April 4), Personal communication.

16. C. Derber, (2001). *The Pursuit of Attention: Power and Ego in Everyday Life* (2nd

ed.). Oxford University Press.

17. T. Keller, (2012). *Center Church: Doing Balanced, Gospel-Centered Ministry in Your City*. Zondervan.

18. V. Johnson, (2021, February 13), The Power of Restorative Conversations, CT3. Retrieved April 20, 2022, from https://www.ct3education.com/2016/03/24/power-restorative-conversations/.

19. Ibid.

20. Ibid.

21. W. White, (2012, January 9), Time to Think: Using Restorative Questions, *International Institute for Restorative Practices*. Retrieved April 20, 2022, from https://www.iirp.edu/news/time-to-think-using-restorative-questions.

22. Warning: Before-and-After Covid Brain Scans Reveal Damage, (2022), Amen Clinics. Retrieved April 23, 2022, from https://www.amenclinics. com/blog/warning-before-and-after-covid-brain-scans-reveal-damage/.

# CHAPTER 8: RESTORING CONNECTION
## Rediscovering the Power of 'We'

Before the pandemic, we joked about introverts who preferred staying home to going out. Memes commented on the unbridled joy introverts feel about canceled plans, the excuses they make to avoid having to socialize, and that during the lockdowns, they were living their "best lives." Cocooning— entertaining and comforting oneself at home— felt like a guilty pleasure. During the pandemic, the general population had to relearn simple pleasures: reading, doing puzzles, crafting, and baking. Pet adoptions and sales of everything pet-related soared. As we set up home offices and spent so much time at home, we soon got bored with our living spaces and started going on a mass national redecorating project. Furniture went on backorder, and prices rose with demand at building supply stores. So-called "preppers" who had been preparing for social collapse for decades enjoyed a heyday, dispensing advice online on living "off the grid."

Many of us found some joy in cocooning, clearing our schedules, and simplifying our commitments. Human beings, though, are fundamentally social creatures. We are herd animals. Psychologist Jordan Bridger points out that the intense loss we feel when we lose someone dear to us is an indication of our deep-seated need for connection:

> Evolutionary psychology frames grief as a design by evolution not simply for release from the pain of a loss but also because we are all hard-wired for connection. When we lose a connection with someone that we love—whether it's a pivotal breakup, divorce,

death, or the loss of a valued pet, the pain within the loss of that connection is also a reminder of the way we are inherently made to be connected to one another.[1]

It wasn't long before most of us missed leaving the house, connecting with coworkers and friends, even the random interactions with strangers we'd previously taken for granted.

> Human beings . . . are fundamentally social creatures.

Long-term isolation isn't healthy. During the lockdowns many ostensibly stable people showed signs of distress, such as hoarding, obsessive-compulsive behavior, and irritability. As the crisis wore on, we saw soaring mental health issues, and the rate of death by suicide rose among young people and people of color.[2] "In the first year of the COVID-19 pandemic, global prevalence of anxiety and depression increased by a massive 25%," according to the World Health Organization.[3] The numbers of those who reported high levels of loneliness jumped, especially among older teens and young adults.[4] Some people acted out in deeply antisocial ways, such as verbally or physically attacking strangers, engaging in domestic abuse, and crime. There have been upticks in everything from reckless driving to "unruly passenger" incidents to car thefts.[5] Racial issues, elections, masking, and vaccination requirements acted as lightning rods for pent-up frustration, bringing large numbers of people to the streets in protest and destructive riots.

We often keep to our own bubbles and opt to spend time with others who think like we do, making schools one of the few places where broad cross-sections of society are still forced to interact. Unfortunately, this has made them an epicenter of the culture wars, with leaders at ground zero.

**BRENÉ BROWN ON CONNECTION AND INVISIBILITY**

Brené Brown eloquently explains the profound importance of connection to our identity and wellbeing:

"Across my research, I define connection as the energy that exists between people when they feel seen, heard, and valued; when they can give and receive without judgment; and when they derive sustenance and strength from the relationship."

"Connection is in our neurobiology. This is why our experiences of disconnection are so painful and why chronic disconnection leads to social isolation, loneliness, and powerlessness."

"Disconnection is often equated with social rejection, social exclusion, and/or social isolation, and these feelings of disconnection actually share the same neural pathways with feelings of physical pain."

"I define invisibility as a function of disconnection and dehumanization, where an individual or group's humanity and relevance are unacknowledged, ignored, and or diminished in value or importance. Given that we are all here to be seen, known, and loved, invisibility is one of the most painful experiences." [6]

My friend Mary, a school leader, called me first thing one morning during the pandemic.

"Sorry to call so early," she said, "but I'm about done. My phone blew up after the school board meeting last night: mask mandates, curriculum, technology, vaccines, parents mad at school staff, you name it. When I got on my computer, it was even worse. I can't take much more!"

I remember that call well because not much shook my even-tempered friend. Mary is one of the most kind, compassionate people I have ever met, and with over 20 years of service in the same district, she is a recognizable and respected name in our school community. One of Mary's strengths has always been her connection with the entire school community. On the phone, though, she was struggling. She could sense the connections in her community dissolving.

The disruption caused by the pandemic was increasing isolation and fears in her school district and in countless others. At the beginning of the shutdown, there had been a conscious effort to maintain fraying connections with students and each other, but as the crisis intensified and the toll of the trauma increased, many people retreated. Years into it, many of us are still struggling to reconnect with each other. We all need some help to repair disrupted connections.

We can begin to move from survival to hope in our school communities when we restore connections by increasing trust and building relationships.

## Understanding Trust

"Trust is defined as choosing to risk making something you value vulnerable to another person's actions," writes Charles Feltman in *The Thin Book of Trust*.[7] Within our teams and school communities, it's impossible to form—or re-form—connections without it. When we want to build back trust, we can think doing so in the three stages of what Joseph Myers terms "The Trust Flywheel": mitigate distrust, engage trust, and test trust. As we move from one to the next, the flywheel revolves, momentum builds, and trust deepens and grows.[8]

- **Mitigate distrust:** This is the first structural element of the flywheel. "Distrust has two 'personalities' that help keep us safe," writes Myers. "The first is the personality of a guard dog. The second is that of a guide dog. For trust to develop, distrust must move from guard dog to guide dog." When the amygdala—the part of the brain that processes emotions—shifts from the guard dog mindset to the guide dog mindset, distrust is mitigated. Myers also emphasizes that we're mitigating distrust—not erasing or eliminating it. "Distrust is always present within healthy trust development."[9]

- **Engage trust:** We begin to engage trust after we've made a mental pro and con list (consciously or subconsciously) of each reason to trust or not. "Our guide dog sits under our feet watching as we carefully list each item for consideration," writes Myers. "The trust process is engaged, and momentum begins to develop."[10]

- **Test trust:** Though the phase of testing trust often takes people by surprise, it's integral to the process. Once we have engaged trust, we need to test it to see if it still holds. "...trust must be tested for it to develop," Myers writes. "It's essential that we maneuver through this stage of trust development. Without it there is no momentum, no developing risk, that increases the energy that's needed for sustained trust."[11]

We can use this knowledge of how trust develops to better understand how our connections strengthen—or weaken.

## CARE Practices To Repair Disrupted Connection

I've developed a practice called CARE—an acronym that stands for Connect, Aware, Respond, and Evaluate/Evolve—that provides a scaffolding to rebuild disrupted connections. As we learn from these strategies, we can refer back to what we learned about how trust develops, as every connection requires a foundation of trust before it can grow.

### CONNECT

We all know that relationships are critical to team success. Building relationships takes time, effort, and skills, and not everyone connects easily or in the same way. During a crisis is when we call upon the relationships fast, wide, and deep that we've already built. We also often use our existing ability to build connections to grow new ones that will help us get through periods of trauma and difficulty.

**Fast Connections:** The skills needed to quickly build rapport come more naturally to some people than others, but they can be cultivated and practiced. We can learn from Dale Carnegie's tried and true tips: build rapport by admitting mistakes, listen genuinely, engage in personal discussions, use humor, be accessible, show concern, and create comfortable communication.[12] When supervisors use nonverbals such as smiling, appropriate touching (handshakes, touching the arm), eye contact, and other affirming actions, team members may feel increased rapport. Remember that these practices are more likely to lead to meaningful connections if we are authentic and sincere, rather than checking them off the list in a mechanical fashion:

**Wide Connections:** We will also benefit from casting a wide relational net, not just calling repeatedly on the people we know best or work with most often. When we lean again and again on the same connections we wear out some of our best people and overlook untapped talent among other staff members. We need a vast relationship network to engage the best talent and weave the whole staff into a unified team.

**Deep Connections:** Deep relationships are the ones in which we can be our genuine selves without guilt and shame—the relationships where we

149

are known and accepted as we are. When we're looking to build deep connections within our teams or in our personal lives, three ingredients are needed:

- **Vulnerability:** Deep relationships require us to step outside of our comfort zones, ask for what we need, be honest about what we're thinking and feeling, and put ourselves out there, accepting what Brené Brown terms the "emotional exposure" that comes with doing so.

- **Shared experience:** Deep relationships are built off of time spent together, both in the vulnerable moments and the lighthearted, fun, and funny ones.

- **Contact:** If you don't stay in touch with someone, it's hard to maintain a deep connection. Contact can look like calling, texting, or spending time together in person. It's more than just reaching out, but remembering what matters to the other person—everything from sharing an inside joke to asking how the meeting they were dreading went.[13]

## AWARE

Awareness is one of the understated skills of a school leader.

One of the best pieces of advice for school leaders is to practice "management by walking around." Most leaders have good intentions about being out on campus but it requires a commitment and scheduling. Consider dividing your building into quadrants. Each day, you will focus on one quadrant. So Monday: quadrant 1, Tuesday: quadrant 2, Wednesday: quadrant 3, Thursday: quadrant 4 and then Friday, you can walk an alternative area or go to where you observed the most need. Despite our best intentions this won't happen every day, but by regularly planning for these times of observation and awareness we can connect with our campuses more deeply, and make ourselves more available to our teams.

This kind of regular observation also gives a keen look into a buildings culture. As educational leaders, we're often focused on detail-oriented tasks and can miss the forest for the trees. Connecting with your team on a regular basis and becoming aware of what is happening across the campus as you walk around will allow you to notice not only what's going well, but to spot signs of trouble early on, when they're much easier to fix.

**12 EARLY WARNING SIGNS YOUR TEAM IS IN TROUBLE**

What are we looking for as we observe the school environment? We certainly want to find examples of things going well to celebrate and individuals to affirm and encourage. We also want to look for warning signs that our teams are in trouble. It helps to watch carefully for the following:

1. Early gut feel that something is off
2. Politics, drama, and turf
3. Disengagement
4. Ignoring elephant issues
5. Problems won't go away
6. Missed milestones
7. Boring meetings with false harmony
8. Safety or quality issues
9. Sidebar meetings after the meeting
10. Frontline folks feel it is us vs. them
11. A weak mission, vision, and values that don't influence behavior
12. Lack of clarity and fuzzy commitments

When we notice, acknowledge, and learn from what is happening on our campuses, we build stronger, more connected teams.

> When we notice, acknowledge, and learn from what is happening on our campuses, we build stronger, more connected teams.

**RESPOND**

The first two steps of CARE—Connect and Aware—are key to ensuring that leaders are able to then *Respond* to campus needs in timely and appropriate ways. The school community needs reassurance that they are valued and that their needs will be met. They don't expect their leaders to have all the answers, but they do expect that our care and concern will be authentic. They need us to *respond* to the situations that arise.

It can be difficult to make quick decisions and communicate them effectively when we live in a culture of distrust and misinformation. Some of the best responses are brief. TedTalks have to be under 18 minutes to hold the audience's attention. Responding clearly, concisely, and cohesively is a balancing act for leaders. One of the greatest mistakes a leader can make is to be secretive and unresponsive. Like anyone else, during times of crisis leaders may go into fight, flight, freeze, or fawn modes. It is okay to not respond immediately while we gather ourselves, but a response is needed, even if it is an imperfect one. The longer we wait, the more time we give the rumor mill to churn, increasing the likelihood that what's communicated won't be the most accurate or appropriate message.

## EVALUATE/EVOLVE

Offering a response is critical, but it is not the end of the process. Evaluation is where we assimilate what we have learned and make course corrections for even more effective responses in the future. We can't afford to wait until a disaster is resolved to review and reflect upon our responses. Evaluation not only assesses whether our responses made the desired impact, but it encompasses self-reflection, which can be an uncomfortable part of the process for us and for our teammates. We might feel that we've already given 110%, so pointing out flaws in what we have done can leave us feeling helpless, as if the best we have to offer is not good enough.

When evaluating a response, here are some questions to reflect upon:

- Was the response appropriate and timely?
- Did it help or hurt the connections in our campus?
- What hit the mark and what missed it?
- How could pitfalls be avoided in the future?
- What needs to occur quickly to amend any missteps?

It's difficult for leaders to evaluate responses that failed, especially ones that failed on a public stage. We can keep in mind Winston Churchill's aphorism: "Perfection is the enemy of progress."

> "Perfection is the enemy of progress."
> - Winston Churchill

To progress, we must evolve. When we evaluate our response and use it to grow, that's the highest form of leadership.

## Restored Connections Lead to Strong Communities

Where do restored connections lead? They lead to a school community where each member feels known and knows they belong. In this connected community we notice when other people are struggling or suffering and offer them compassion and support. We encourage one another and cheer together over our wins. We balance out each other's strengths and weaknesses. And we work together for the good of the students we serve.

## SURVIVING THE STORM

### REFLECTION QUESTIONS

1. What CARE (Connect, Aware, Respond, and Evaluate/Evolve) element is a strength of yours as a leader? What element might be a weakness?

2. On a scale of 1-10, rate the trust level on your campus before and after the pandemic. Are they within two points? If not, to what do you attribute the change?

3. How well known and utilized are the strengths of the staff and school community?

4. As a leader, how have you intentionally set a climate that helps build connections between peers and leaders?

### STRAIGHTFORWARD SURVIVAL

When we experience disruption, sometimes we need simple ideas for taking a next, practical step forward. If you are unsure of where to start, choose one of these ideas from the chapter:

- Celebrate and be grateful for daily accomplishments.

- Implement a personal/professional check-in at the beginning of meetings or phone calls and discuss struggles and celebrations.

- Plan time together with someone in your "circle of five"—the five people you can talk to about your strengths and weaknesses.

# ENDNOTES

1.  Jordan Bridger (George Elerick) - American Psychological Association. (2022, March 1). *We Grieve So We Can Connect.* LinkedIn. Retrieved April 4, 2022, from https://www.linkedin.com/pulse/we-grieve-so-can-connect-american-psychological-association/.

2.  Rodriguez, A. (2021, November 4). Overall Suicide Rates Fell During COVID-19 but Increased Among Young and People of Color, Study Finds. USA TODAY. Retrieved April 29, 2022, from https://eu.usatoday.com/story/news/health/2021/11/04/covid-despite-mental-health-crisis-study-shows-suicide-rate-declined/6248176001/.

3.  COVID-19 *Pandemic Triggers 25% Increase in Prevalence of Anxiety and Depression Worldwide.* (2022, March 2). World Health Organization. Retrieved April 29, 2022, from https://www.who.int/news/item/02-03-2022-covid-19-pandemic-triggers-25-increase-in-prevalence-of-anxiety-and-depression-worldwide.

4.  Walsh, C. (2021, February 17). Young Adults Hardest Hit by Loneliness During Pandemic, Study Finds. *Harvard Gazette.* Retrieved April 29, 2022, from https://news.harvard.edu/gazette/story/2021/02/young-adults-teens-loneliness-mental-health-coronavirus-covid-pandemic.

5.  Khazan, O. (2022, April 1). Why People Are Acting So Weird. *The Atlantic.* Retrieved April 29, 2022, from https://www.theatlantic.com/politics/archive/2022/03/antisocial-behavior-crime-violence-increase-pandemic/627076/

6.  Brown, B. (2022). *Atlas of the Heart: Mapping Meaningful Connection and the Language of Human Experience.* Random House Inc. 169, 171, 176.

7.  Feltman, C. (2021). *The Thin Book of Trust: An Essential Primer for Building Trust at Work* (2nd ed.). Thin Book Publishing.

8.  Myers, J. (n.d.). Discovering the Trust Flywheel. In *Trust Me: Discovering Trust in a Culture of Distrust.* Not Yet Published.

9.  Ibid.

10. Ibid.

11. Ibid.

12. Carnegie, D. (1998). How to Win Friends & Influence People. Pocket Books.

13. *Three Ingredients for Deep Friendships.* (2020, February 15). Momentous Institute. Retrieved April 30, 2022, from https://momentousinstitute.org/blog/three-ingredients-for-deep-friendships.

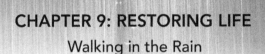

## CHAPTER 9: RESTORING LIFE
### Walking in the Rain

**W**hen Brad and Wendy Meece told their families they were moving to Seattle, they got predictable reactions: "Oh my God, it rains there ALL THE TIME. Aren't you going to be so depressed?" But, truth be told, the Meeces actually *liked* rainy days. In fact, that's how they met, walking in the park on a wet and gloomy October afternoon in Chicago. Maybe it was weird. But it was a weirdness that they shared and liked about each other.

As it turned out, summers in Seattle were often surprisingly dry and sunny, but also quite short. Like the locals, Brad and Wendy tended to pack those few weeks with outdoor activities and socializing. In winter their routine became more "normal" and productive as day after day of misty rain and sometimes hard downpours drove the focus of activity indoors. Nevertheless, the rain didn't stop them from going to work, out to eat, or for long walks on the lush, mossy trails of a northern Pacific rainforest. Some days it did get a little old, but they navigated those times as part of the rhythm of imperfect living. On balance, even in the wettest months, their good days outweighed the bad.

Trauma is not fun. Grief is not romantic. Unending crisis is not the lifestyle any of us would choose. I don't share the Meeces' story to diminish the depth of the grief and trauma each of us has experienced—if not in the pandemic, then in innumerable personal experiences that may hang over our heads like rain clouds. I also don't want to encourage fatalistic defeatism, suggesting that things will never be better so we must learn to live as we are. I do, however, want to acknowledge that crisis and the attendant trauma it can bring are recurring parts of life, and for that reason, we must develop the resilience to live and grow in the storm, not only to live through it. And in so doing, we'll not only *survive* but *thrive*.

## A New Normal?

Much like 9/11 changed air travel forever, the pandemic and the mayhem that surrounds it ushered in new forms of working, going to school, and everyday living. These are not an aberration from normal, they are the new normal.

When the mandatory quarantines first went into place, I contacted Dr. Jeff Jernigan, an expert on stress and fatigue disorders. We discussed where we were and how those of us guiding school communities could lead effectively in the weeks and months to follow. In his words, "We are facing wartime conditions." He went on to describe the aftershocks that companies, institutions, and families would face in the coming months. "Our first objective is to help leaders treat this shock to the nation not as an event, but as a process," he advised.

Back then, those of us who recognized we were entering uncharted territory wondered what the long process ahead of us would bring. *Can't we just get back to normal?* is a sentiment that echoes what many are feeling. But when we encounter stress, trauma, and difficulty, we have to ask ourselves: Is getting back to normal really what we want? Will we choose to "waste" this crisis by simply restoring what existed before? Or, do we want to use it to put into place a process of reflection and improvement in the programs, processes, procedures, and practices of our schools? If the crisis has exposed fundamental weaknesses in the way we do education, isn't this the time for us to repair or replace the foundations? Isn't that ultimately a better response than attempting to put things back the way they were before?

> "Our first objective is to help leaders treat this shock to the nation not as an event, but as a process." — Dr. Jeff Jernigan

## Legacy, Liberating, Letting Go

Ideally, the process of post-traumatic leading is an opportunity to let go of dysfunctional practices and find new ones that will better serve the goals of our organization and the needs of our students. When navigating trauma, I encourage school leaders to evaluate everything they're doing through the lens of effectiveness rather than emotion. Some questions we might ask along those lines: Is this part of our school legacy? Can it be liberated? Does it need to be let go? Here is some clarification:

- **Legacy** practices are an integral part of the school culture and still serve a useful purpose. For example, recognizing strengths and encouraging collaboration will likely be a legacy you want to continue in your school's culture.

- **Liberating** refers to freeing valuable practices from constraints that no longer serve a purpose. It's welcoming freedom and expansiveness to what we are currently doing. For instance, Multi-Tiered Systems of Support (MTSS) serve students well in the academic arena but miss the mark in behavioral and emotional skill development. This process might be liberated to meet non-academic student needs by expanding it to include time during the school day to reinforce positive behavior support strategies or build student learning communities.

- **Letting Go** means what you think it does. We need to assess what it's time to say goodbye to. Do our instructional programs still meet the needs of our students? Does the data show that students are making gains? Do our programs offer a technology component? Do they authentically integrate future-ready skills such as collaboration, critical thinking, and problem-solving, or is it more "drill and kill" to reinforce concepts? Keeping an ineffective program is detrimental and wastes valuable time.

One district I worked with started this evaluation process with their school-wide curriculum support program. They came up with the most objective rubric they could and anonymously polled teachers and other staff to determine whether the program was being used and was effective. They learned that very few teachers used the program because of a lack of awareness and training. The committee asked a few teachers to try the program to offer some additional perspectives. In this case, they decided to liberate the program rather than letting it go. They went through a process that allowed them to identify the best parts of the program and ensure that teachers understood and were trained on those parts.

This is a great example of taking the things off teachers' plates that are not working while putting on their plates what will increase their capacity. Collective leader and teacher efficacy can be game-changers. This efficacy builds a climate on strengths instead of weaknesses, increasing cohesiveness and professionalism. It will lead to a culture change where your school community can be a symbiotic ecosystem of learning and wellness.

## A Lighthouse to Post-Traumatic Growth

An old anecdote tells of a fully-loaded freighter navigating the sea on a stormy night with low visibility. Spotting a light directly in front of them, the captain radioed to the light: "Attention: unknown vessel, we are a 100,000-ton cargo ship headed directly for you, adjust your course 45 degrees to starboard immediately!" To this, the light replied, "We are a lighthouse. Adjust your course 45 degrees to starboard immediately." In our context, how can we transition from being a ship struggling to stay on course to a lighthouse that withstands the worst storms, and guides others to a safe place for future growth?

> How can we transition from being a ship struggling to stay on course to a lighthouse that withstands the worst storms, and guides others to a safe place for future growth?

The school community, staff, and students look to their leadership for validation. When that validation or presence is absent, we see decreased trust, declining morale, and disengagement. When validation rewards courageous growth efforts, leaders will see those behaviors increase. You want your school community to see you as a pillar of trust and stability, even if you don't always feel that way inside. Most leaders I've talked with are excited but apprehensive about what school will look like when the storm has passed. We're all full of ideas, but where do we start?

Throughout this book, we've talked about various disruptions and provided research and suggestions for ways to address them. Each of these disruptions carries the potential to lead a school community toward post-traumatic growth—but that growth doesn't always happen quickly, and the aftereffects of trauma can last a long time. To avoid discouragement, we can consider what post-traumatic growth looks like, along with some testimonies from educational professionals who have begun to see that growth.

Connection
Resilience
Focus
Control
Capacity
Confidence
Communication

*A lighthouse to post-traumatic growth*

## Straightforward Survival

Like friends sheltering during a storm as it subsides, you and I have ventured out of our shelter and walked around the neighborhood together, surveying the damage and starting to think about how to recover from it. By no means has this book definitively explored all the possible features of post-traumatic growth, but it has focused on the areas of disruption that trauma inflicts, and thus, the areas that most need healing and growth. I hope what has been offered here has encouraged you and will inspire you to do further research into the areas most beneficial to yourself and your situation. Let's look back at where we've been, think about what post-traumatic growth might look like in these circumstances, and consider some comments from friends who have started down this path of growth.

We've seen how chaos has disrupted our *lives* with the trauma of a mass disaster event, and that such events trigger predictable reaction patterns.

## SURVIVING THE STORM

Being aware of the stage of trauma we and others are in can help us have realistic expectations and continue to make progress toward our goals. Some evidence of post-traumatic growth we can expect in our lives includes engaging in serious self-reflection; acknowledging that a serious problem exists; being able to identify how our circumstances line up with established patterns of mass disaster response; and becoming more receptive to learning about effective responses to our circumstances. Regarding recovery from a disrupted life, Angela comments:

> Your training was the first time I had seen the stages of processing a mass disaster event. I applied it to my career change that coincided with the pandemic but wasn't directly related to it. I could actually see how each of those stages had been going on in my life and wished I had realized it at the time. It would have made a world of difference. I've been talking to my husband about it and even though it wasn't presented as something to understand marriage, ours is kind of a disaster and it seems to fit.

Our *capacity* has also been disrupted by grief and trauma. We normally try on different "stories" or stages of grief until we can reach a point of acceptance and integrate a loss into our lives. Trauma can short-circuit a healthy grieving process and cause us to get stuck unproductively at a particular stage of grief. How do we recognize growth in our disrupted capacity? We might see a school community that does a better job of recognizing signs of grief and trauma and supporting those who are enduring them. We could also see increased acceptance of sadness, anger, and other unpleasant emotions as healthy parts of a grieving process that should not be rushed. Jeannine found my discussion of grief with her faculty helpful:

> I didn't realize how grief was affecting us all individually and collectively. Many teachers had their own personal concerns as well as anxiety about students returning with major traumatic effects. A lot of the returning students have really low motivation. Keeping in mind the dynamics of grief and trauma has helped our teachers be more understanding of themselves and their students and to employ strategies that have helped students keep moving forward, even if it's just an inch at a time. I think if we hadn't realized this we may have tried to rush the students back to "normal" and done even more damage, when they really needed a safe place to heal.

## HABITS OF MIND

Thriving in post-traumatic growth includes developing problem-solving strategies that help us behave intelligently when we are confronted with a problem that does not have an immediate solution. Based on studies of people of all backgrounds with proven problem-solving skills, Art Costa and Bena Kallick have suggested 16 Habits of Mind that can increase our intellectual resources when facing thorny problems. These take time to cultivate, and practice to implement consistently and well, but the payoff will be greater confidence when facing the unknown and an expanded ability to create solutions that are powerful, effective, and long-lasting.[1] The Institute for Habits of Mind (habitsofmindinstitute.org) offers numerous useful resources for leaders, teachers, parents, and students to increase their mastery of these habits.

1. Persisting
2. Managing Impulsivity
3. Listening with Understanding and Empathy
4. Thinking Flexibly
5. Thinking about Thinking
6. Striving for Accuracy
7. Questioning and Posing Problems
8. Applying Past Knowledge to New Situations
9. Thinking and Communicating with Clarity & Precision
10. Gathering Data Through All Senses
11. Creating, Imagining, Innovating
12. Responding with Wonderment and Awe
13. Taking Responsible Risks
14. Finding Humor
15. Thinking Interdependently
16. Remaining Open to Continuous Learning

*The Habits of Mind. (2022, February 7). The Institute for Habits of Mind. Retrieved April 4, 2022, from https://www.habitsofmindinstitute.org/learning-the-habits/.*

## SURVIVING THE STORM

*Focus* is another significant area of disruption in a major crisis. With limited time, energy and resources, where do we focus our energy and attention for maximum impact? We saw that these decisions require community buy-in, that we need to target some low-hanging fruit to build momentum, and that we need longer-term goals and strategies that will move us toward a much better future than we could dream possible today. A school growing in its ability to focus properly will engage in co-creation of plans to propel the school toward a common vision; a climate and culture that becomes more about "we" instead of "me;" and collaboration between the staff to meet the needs of the whole child. According to Marc,

> The constant firefighting to put out urgent but not important tasks takes a toll on what I can truly spend quality time on. I'm looking more intentionally at what I have to handle and what can be delegated. I'm looking back at priorities and trying to ensure what I'm spending time on is what I should be. I'm using the power of the plan and building trust in my campus by growing leaders within. It is changing the climate and even the culture of our school. It's still a work in progress, but it feels good to see it moving in the right direction.

*Resilience* is a crucial quality if we are to bounce back from the blows of life, but it can become disrupted after a series of major hits. One of the best inspirations for resiliency is to give ourselves credit for how we have already demonstrated it all our lives. A workable strategy for recovering resilience is to take solid breaks interspersed with sprints using manageable challenges. Encouraging signs of growth in resilience include a culture of genuine positivity; utilization of trauma-informed design in the classroom; and emotion-based and problem-based coping strategies being developed and utilized appropriately. Sophie responded to these ideas like this:

> It was like our school had a switch—no matter what was said, someone put a positive spin on it. Now I have a term for it: "toxic positivity." It became the answer to every problem and it just wasn't. It seemed positive but it actually alienated people because they didn't feel heard or taken seriously. Even those who were the most resilient began to tire of every off-hand comment being touted as a solution. Today we are still positive but we've made it safe to temper that positivity with reality that allows us to look at

issues seriously and use coping styles and collaborative problem-solving to meet our goals.

When our **confidence** is disrupted, getting back on our feet is only partially about recovering our skills or learning new ones. It's also about believing in ourselves, that we are able and willing to do the job, and that our institutions are up to the challenge. There is much we can do at the micro, meso, macro, and mega levels to restore this confidence, and even in an unsupportive workplace we can take healthy individual actions that can help restore our own confidence. A school growing in confidence will feature teacher wellness as a part of the campus culture; experience reduced friction between staff members; and welcome teacher-led innovation rather than fearing it. Daniel shared,

> The BE CALM strategy was easy to remember and helped me through an uncomfortable conversation with a staff member this week. It's helped me learn to model the behavior I wanted to see in my staff. Also, it was clarifying for me to think through teacher requests for wellness activities that meet their needs as something that is beneficial to the whole school climate.

It can be difficult and uncomfortable to exercise **control** when it has been disrupted by turbulent times. Understanding that complete control is impossible, we noted it is usually possible to exercise various degrees of influence that, cumulatively with the efforts of others, even across generations, can make long-lasting change. We also looked at what we always have the ability to control: ourselves, and our responses to our circumstances. In a school setting, control exerted with a light, strategic touch can result in increased engagement of students, teachers, and leaders; deeper student ownership of their own learning; and greater creativity to enhance learning. Here's a description in Anya's words:

> As much as we wanted to be able to control the chaos of the pandemic, it was a hollow effort. Ultimately it boiled down to the importance of engagement through relationships. Once we have the relationships, it becomes easier to keep students engaged. I've worked on this model with my teachers and have used the freedom in the framework to give them ownership. Now in our classrooms, teachers are allowing students to have more voice, choice, and ownership over their own learning. It has led to better

connections. We are able to see the flywheel in motion and it has a life of its own.

Chaotic circumstances can severely disrupt **communication**, interfering both with our ability to send clear messages and others' ability to receive them. Communicating during a crisis requires sensitivity to the cognitive processing challenges that traumatized people experience, rebuilding trust to communicate effectively. Post-traumatic growth in this area looks like restorative communication that builds relationships—we're not only back to our pre-rupture state, but our relationships are better and stronger than they were before. In Marquetta's experience,

> We tried everything possible to communicate. The problem is just because it is said the same way, it's not always understood the same way. When we were all virtual, we started smaller breakout rooms online to help each staff member feel heard and ask questions. We let each member of the team be a facilitator and we met a day or two before so they felt comfortable having the conversation. We let everyone know that some conversations would be led with the head and others with the heart: either "tell us how you feel first;" or "tell us logically what you think." This really helped people who processed things differently from others, so everybody could feel like they had something to contribute. We liked it enough to continue something like it after going back to in-person meetings.

Trauma can disrupt vital **connections** to others at the time we need them most. Fear and hurt cause us to isolate, miscommunicate, and misinterpret others' well-meaning gestures. Lack of connection saps us of our confidence, leaves us feeling powerless and confused, and makes us feel it's pointless to try anymore. Restored connection, perhaps more than anything else, is the key to post-traumatic recovery. We can focus on building connections fast, wide, and deep, recognizing that all levels of connection rely on a foundation of trust. The use of CARE strategies to increase awareness and develop connections will lead toward deepened relationships at all levels of the school community. Karen sees it like this:

> I was 100% certain that post-traumatic growth would look like addressing academic gaps but it's not; it's been creating connections not just between the students but our staff as well. I had no idea how much connection mattered until we didn't have it.

Now that is a major focus: building that connection first. The CARE strategy has helped me understand the importance of each stage to build trust and keep the connection strong.

## From Trauma to Transformation

Trauma disturbs our fundamental life searches in ways that cut us to the core. We experience a sense of vertigo as core pursuits of identity, significance, belonging, and hope are threatened. With all that's at stake, we have no choice but to fight through the crisis—but what do we have to look forward to on the other side? How will we emerge? Scarred for life, stronger for life, or a little of both?

Neil Gaiman wrote, "Fairy tales are more than true, not because they tell us that dragons exist, but because they tell us that dragons can be beaten." We each struggle with our personal dragons, but if we do the hard work to grow through trauma, we can beat them, emerging transformed on the other side. Elisabeth Kübler-Ross memorably wrote,

> The most beautiful people we have known are those who have known defeat, known suffering, known struggle, known loss, and have found their way out of the depths. These persons have an appreciation, a sensitivity, and an understanding of life that fills them with compassion, gentleness, and a deep loving concern. Beautiful people do not just happen.[2]

"Fairy tales are more than true, not because they tell us that dragons exist, but because they tell us that dragons can be beaten." - Neil Gaiman

On the other side of trauma is transformation into a better you. Less innocent, perhaps. Well aware that the world is a dangerous place that buffets us with losses. More appreciative of the fragility of life. More respectful of the unstoppable power of the ocean of events engulfing this world. But you are also likely to become more quietly confident that you have the strength and fortitude to get through those losses, and the courage to find joy in the midst of them—a joy that transcends circumstances, rather than being drowned by them. That is the kind of person we would all be glad to follow.

## SURVIVING THE STORM

To all who are reading these words, Well done! You are surviving the storm of a generation. You are here, now. You might feel like you're barely making it—but you're progressing more than you realize. A college dean speaking to an uncertain young doctoral candidate once said, "In this field we have a special term we use for people who just barely finished their dissertation and just managed to eke through their doctoral defense by the skin of their teeth. We call them Doctor." Similarly, we have a special term for someone like you—someone who may feel like you are just barely hanging on, just barely got through the crisis with your sanity intact. We call a person like you Survivor.

> The things we're trying to do are not easy. If they were, others would have already done them.

**REFLECTION QUESTIONS**

1. In your life, what evidence can you already identify of progress toward post-traumatic growth in each of the following domains:

   - Appreciation of life

   - Relationships with others

   - New possibilities

   - Personal strength

   - Spiritual change

2. For those areas where you cannot yet identify any evidence of growth, what practical steps can you take to get the process moving?

**STRAIGHTFORWARD SURVIVAL**

At the beginning of each day check in with as many adults as possible (teachers, parents, support staff).Practice a self-reflection process at the end of conversations. Ask yourself:

- Was the response appropriate and timely?

- Did it help or hurt the connections on our campus?

- What hit the mark and what missed it?

- How could pitfalls be avoided in the future?

## ENDNOTES

1.  What Are the Habits of Mind? (2022, January 19). TeachThought. Retrieved April 4, 2022, from https://www.teachthought.com/pedagogy/what-are-the-habits-of-mind/.

2.  Kübler-Ross, E. (1975). Death: the final stage of growth. Hoboken, NJ: Wiley & Sons.

# BIBLIOGRAPHY

2021 Unruly Passenger Data. (2022, February 22). Federal Aviation Administration. Retrieved February 28, 2022, from https://www.faa.gov/data_research/passengers_cargo/unruly_passengers/2021_archive/.

Allen, J. (2022, January 15). Superintendent Struggle: Covid-19 Pandemic, Incivility Likely to Blame for Exodus of School Leaders, Experts Say. *Spokesman.com*. Retrieved March 23, 2022, from https://www.spokesman.com/stories/2022/jan/16/superintendent-struggle-covid-19-pandemic-incivili/.

American Psychological Association (2009). *Publication Manual of the American Psychological Association* (6th Ed.). Washington, DC.: Author. (2nd printing).

Bandura, A. (1977). Self-Efficacy: Toward a Unifying Theory of Behavioral Change. *Psychological Review, 84*(2), 191–215.

*The Bible: New International Version.* (1984). International Bible Society.

Black, J. (2020, June 22). Disrupted Focus and Lower Energy are the Brain's Response to the Pandemic. Duke University, Department of Psychology & Neuroscience. Retrieved March 23, 2022, from https://psychandneuro.duke.edu/news/disrupted-focus-and-lower-energy-are-brain%E2%80%99s-response-pandemic.

Boyd-Franklin, N., & Bry, B. H. (2001). *Reaching Out In Family Therapy: Home-Based, School, and Community Interventions.* New York: Guilford.

Bridger, J. (2022, March 1). We Grieve So We Can Connect. *LinkedIn.* Retrieved April 4, 2022, from https://www.linkedin.com/pulse/we-grieve-so-can-connect-american-psychological-association.

Bried, E. (2015, May 16). What It's Like To Be Me: I Was Crushed By An 80-Foot Wave. *SELF.* Retrieved March 8, 2022, from https://www.self.com/story/what-its-like-to-be-me-i-was-crushed-by-an-80-foot-wave.

Brown, B. (2022). *Atlas of the Heart: Mapping Meaningful Connection and the Language of Human Experience.* Random House Inc.

Brunetti, M. (n.d.). Here's How to Help Kids Master the 3 Types of Self-Control. *The Instillery.* Retrieved April 18, 2022, from https://www.the-instillery.com/story/heres-how-to-help-kids-master-the-3-types-of-self-control.

Carnegie, D. (1913). *How to Win Friends and Influence People.* The World's Work.

Coleman, Kali. (2021, November 2). You Could Get Banned from Flying for Doing This. *Best Life.* Retrieved February 28, 2022, from https://bestlifeonline.com/banned-from-flying-news/.

Costa, A., & Kallick, B. (2008). *Leading and Learning with Habits of Mind: 16 Characteristics for Success.* Alexandria, VA: ASCD.

Covey, S. R. (2020). *The 7 Habits of Highly Effective People.* Simon & Schuster UK Ltd.

The Covid Cloud Is Starting to Lift–but Two Years On, Its Legacy of Grief Lingers.

(2022, March 12). *The Guardian*. Retrieved April 4, 2022, from https://www.theguardian.com/us-news/2022/mar/12/covid-pandemic-two-years-later.

Dash, M. (2013, January 28). For 40 years, This Russian Family was Cut Off from All Human Contact, Unaware of World War II. Smithsonian.com. Retrieved March 16, 2022, from https://www.smithsonianmag.com/history/for-40-years-this-russian-family-was-cut-off-from-all-human-contact-unaware-of-world-war-ii-7354256/.

Dass-Brailsford, P. (2007). *A Practical Approach to Trauma*. Sage.

Davidson, et al. (2008). *A Practical Guide to Recovery-Oriented Practice: Tools for Transforming Mental Health Care*. New York: Oxford University Press.

Deitchman, A. (2022). Wait, What? On Social Network Use and Attention. *Applied Psychology OPUS*. Retrieved March 24, 2022, from https://wp.nyu.edu/steinhardt-appsych_opus/wait-what-on-social-network-use-and-attention/.

Donohoo, J., Hattie, J., & Eells, R. (2018). The Power of Collective Efficacy. *Educational Leadership*, 75(6), 40–44.

Druckenmiller, R. (2022, March 10). What's Beneath Burnout: Finding Meaning in the Mess [web log]. Retrieved April 4, 2022, from https://www.linkedin.com/pulse/whats-beneath-burnout-finding-meaning-mess-rachel-druckenmiller-.

Ferrazzi, K., & Morken, C. C. (2022, March 17). 3 Practices That Set Resilient Teams Apart. *Harvard Business Review*. Retrieved April 4, 2022, from https://hbr.org/2022/03/3-practices-that-set-resilient-teams-apart.

Fifth Stage of Grief: Acceptance. *eCondolence.com*. (n.d.). Retrieved March 1, 2022, from https://www.econdolence.com/learning-center/grief-and-coping/the-stages-of-grief/fifth-stage-of-grief-acceptance/.

First Stage of Grief: Denial. *eCondolence.com*. (n.d.). Retrieved February 28, 2022, from https://www.econdolence.com/learning-center/grief-and-coping/the-stages-of-grief/first-stage-of-grief-denial/.

Fourth Stage of Grief: Depression. *eCondolence.com*. (n.d.). Retrieved March 1, 2022, from https://www.econdolence.com/learning-center/grief-and-coping/the-stages-of-grief/fourth-stage-of-grief-depression/.

Fowler, S. (2019). *Master Your Motivation: Three Scientific Truths for Achieving Your Goals*. Berrett-Koehler Publishers, Incorporated.

Gabrielle Scarlett, A. G. (n.d.). Adverse childhood experiences. Retrieved March 1, 2022, from https://www.ncsl.org/research/health/adverse-childhood-experiences-aces.aspx#.

Gill, N. (2019, December 9). Council post: The Importance of Trauma-Informed Design. *Forbes*. Retrieved March 29, 2022, from https://www.forbes.com/sites/forbesnonprofitcouncil/2019/12/09/the-importance-of-trauma-informed-design/?sh=1b7528a66785.

Gottman, J. M., & Silver, N. (2018). *The Seven Principles for Making Marriage Work.* Orion Spring.

Greene, G. J., et al. (2006). A Solution-Focused Approach for Supporting Mental Health Recovery with Consumers Who Have a Severe Mental Disability. *Families in Society,* 87(3), 339-350.

Gruenert, S. (2008). School Culture, School Climate: They Are Not the Same Thing. *Principal,* 56–59.

The Habits of Mind. (2022, February 7). The Institute for Habits of Mind. Retrieved April 4, 2022, from https://www.habitsofmindinstitute.org/learning-the-habits/.

Hattie, J. (2016, July). Mindframes and Maximizers. 3rd Annual Visible Learning Conference held in Washington, D.C.

Helping Someone with PTSD. (2022, March 16). *HelpGuide.org.* Retrieved April 5, 2022, from https://www.helpguide.org/articles/ptsd-trauma/helping-someone-with-ptsd.htm.

Hidden Signs of Depression: How to Spot Them and What to Do. *Medical News Today.* Retrieved March 1, 2022, from https://www.medicalnewstoday.com/articles/325513.

Hougaard, R. (2018, March 7). Self-Awareness Can Help Leaders More Than an MBA Can. *Harvard Business Review.* Retrieved April 18, 2022, from https://hbr.org/2018/01/self-awareness-can-help-leaders-more-than-an-mba-can.

How common is PTSD in adults? (2018, September 13). Va.gov: Veterans Affairs. Retrieved April 4, 2022, from https://www.ptsd.va.gov/understand/common/common_adults.asp.

How Trauma Can Affect Communication. (2021, January 28). Sana Counseling. Retrieved April 5, 2022, from https://sanacounselling.ca/blog/how-trauma-can-affect-communication.

How Trauma-Informed Communication Improves Workplace Culture. (n.d.). FEI Behavioral Health. Retrieved April 6, 2022, from https://www.feinet.com/assets/uploads/2020/01/WPQ120_Trauma-Informed-Communication.pdf.

Hudgens, R., et al. (2020, September 1). Helping You Help Others. *PositivePsychology.com.* Retrieved March 28, 2022, from https://positivepsychology.com/.

Iati, M. (2021, December 25). The Pandemic Has Caused Nearly Two Years of Collective Trauma. Many People Are Near a Breaking Point. *The Washington Post.* Retrieved April 4, 2022, from https://www.washingtonpost.com/health/2021/12/24/collective-trauma-public-outbursts/.

Juneja, A. (n.d.). A Lesson from the Choluteca Bridge During COVID-19. *Digital Healthcare Patient Engagement Platform.* Retrieved March 24, 2022, from https://www.patientbond.com/blog/a-lesson-from-the-choluteca-bridge-during-covid-19.

Kagan, R., & Schlosberg, S. (1989). *Families in Perpetual Crisis*. New York, NY: Norton.

Kallick, B., & Zmuda, A. (2017). *Students at the Center: Personalizing Learning and Habits of Mind*. Alexandria, VA: ASCD.

Kohll, A. (2021, December 10). 25 Ways to Cut Employee Stress and Boost Productivity. *Forbes*. Retrieved April 11, 2022, from https://www.forbes.com/sites/alankohll/2017/02/22/25-ways-to-cut-employee-stress-and-boost-productivity/.

Kruger, F. (2018, July 13). The Role of Consolidation Theory in Learning. *Psychology of Education*. Retrieved March 25, 2022, from https://psy3850c.wordpress.com/2018/07/13/the-role-of-consolidation-theory-in-learning/.

La Greca, A. M., Silverman, W. K., Vernberg, E. M., & Roberts, M. C. (2002). *Helping Children Cope with Disaster and Terrorism*. Washington, DC: American Psychological Association.

Landau, J., Mittal, M., & Wieling, E. (2008). Linking Human Systems: Strengthening Individuals, Families, and Communities in the Wake of Mass Trauma. *Journal of Marital and Family Therapy*, 34, 193-209.

Liner, A. (n.d.). The 5 Stages of Grief and How to Get Through Them. Retrieved February 28, 2022, from https://www.fluxpsychology.com/blog/the-5-stages-of-grief-and-how-to-get-through-them.

Lloyd, M. (2019, October 18). 'Happy to Chat' Benches: The Woman Getting Strangers to Talk. *BBC News*. Retrieved March 1, 2022, from https://www.bbc.com/news/uk-wales-50000204.

Madsen, W. C. (2009). Collaborative Helping: A Practice Framework for Family-Centered Services. *Family Process*, 48, 103-116.

The Main Idea. (2021, September 15). Retrieved April 4, 2022, from https://www.themainidea.net/get-inspired/.

Majority of US Faculty Members Help Students Deal with Mental Health Issues—But Few Are Trained to Do So. (2021, April 15). Boston University. Retrieved March 1, 2022, from https://www.bu.edu/articles/2021/majority-of-us-faculty-members-help-students-deal-with-mental-health-issues-but-few-are-trained-to-do-so/.

Manes, S. (2021, January 20). Making Sure Emotional Flooding Doesn't Capsize Your Relationship. The Gottman Institute. Retrieved March 25, 2022, from https://www.gottman.com/blog/making-sure-emotional-flooding-doesnt-capsize-your-relationship/.

McGoldrick, M., Giordano, J., & Garcia-Preto, N. (Eds.) (2005). *Ethnicity and Family Therapy* (3rd Ed.). Guilford.

McInerny, N. (n.d.). We Don't "Move On" from Grief. We Move Forward with It. *TED Talk*. Retrieved April 4, 2022, from https://www.ted.com/talks/nora_mcinerny_we_don_t_move_on_from_grief_we_move_forward_with_it/.

McMurdock, M. (2022, February 20). School Leader Crisis: Overwhelmed by Mounting Mental Health Issues and Public Distrust, a 'Mass Exodus' of Principals Could Be Coming. Retrieved April 4, 2022, from https://www.the74million.org/article/school-leaders-crisis-overwhelmed-by-mounting-mental-health-issues-public-distrust-mass-exodus-of-principals-could-be-coming/.

Miller, M. R., Latham, B., Baird, K., & Kinder, M. (2020). *Whole: What Teachers Need to Help Students Thrive.* Jossey-Bass.

Miller, R. (2022, March 8). Personal communication.

Montenegro, A. (2017). Understanding the Concept of Agentic Engagement. Retrieved April 6, 2022, from https://www.researchgate.net/publication/316605699_Understanding_the_Concept_of_Agentic_Engagement.

Myers, J. (2022, April 4). Personal communication.

Napier, N. (1994). *Getting Through the Day: Strategies for Adults Hurt as Children.* Norton.

Nunez, K. (2020, February 21). Fight, Flight, or Freeze: How We Respond to Threats. *Healthline.* Retrieved March 25, 2022, from https://www.healthline.com/health/mental-health/fight-flight-freeze#in-the-body.

The Opportunity Myth. (n.d.). Retrieved April 6, 2022, from https://opportunitymyth.tntp.org/.

Pazzanese, C. (2016, July 12). The High Price of Workplace Stress. *Harvard Gazette.* Retrieved April 11, 2022, from https://news.harvard.edu/gazette/story/2016/07/the-high-price-of-workplace-stress/.

Perry, B., & Szalavitz, M. (2006). *The Boy Who Was Raised as a Dog: And Other Stories from a Child Psychiatrist Notebook.* Basic Books.

Preidt, R. (n.d.). Injuries from Ocean Waves More Common than Thought. *WebMD.* Retrieved March 8, 2022, from https://www.webmd.com/children/news/20130623/injuries-from-ocean-waves-more-common-than-thought.

Protect Your Brain from Stress. (2021, February 15). *Harvard Health.* Retrieved April 5, 2022, from https://www.health.harvard.edu/mind-and-mood/protect-your-brain-from-stress.

Rock, D., & Swartz, J. (2006). The Neuroscience of Leadership. *Strategy+Business, 43,* 8.

Rogers, S. (2021, December 10). The Role of Technology in the Evolution of Communication. *Forbes.* Retrieved March 2, 2022, from https://www.forbes.com/sites/solrogers/2019/10/15/the-role-of-technology-in-the-evolution-of-communication/?sh=43a9c5d0493b.

Rojano, R. (2004). The Practice of Community Family Therapy. *Family Process, 43,* 59-77.

Rosen, Andrew, et al. (2021, August 23). What Is Trauma? The Center for Treatment of Anxiety and Mood Disorders. Retrieved March 1, 2022, from https://center-foranxietydisorders.com/what-is-trauma/.

Rotter, J. B. (1966). Generalized Expectancies for Internal Versus External Control of Reinforcement. *Psychological Monographs: General and Applied, 80*(1), 1–28. https://doi.org/10.1037/h0092976.

Schaefer, F. C., Schaefer, C. A., Carr, K. F., Hamel, L. A., & Shaum, S. E. (2012). Normal Reactions After Trauma. In *Trauma & resilience: A Handbook: Effectively Supporting Those Who Serve God.* Essay, Condeo Press.

The School Principal as Leader: Guiding Schools to Better Teaching and Learning. (2013). The Wallace Foundation.

Second Stage of Grief: Anger. (n.d.). *eCondolence.com.* Retrieved February 28, 2022, from https://www.econdolence.com/learning-center/grief-and-coping/the-stag-es-of-grief/second-stage-of-grief-anger/.

Smith, M. (2022, March 16). Helping Someone with PTSD. *HelpGuide.org.* Retrieved April 5, 2022, from https://www.helpguide.org/articles/ptsd-trauma/helping-someone-with-ptsd.htm.

Sprenkle, D. H. (Ed.) (2002). *Effectiveness Research in Marriage and Family Therapy.* Alexandria, VA: American Association for Marriage and Family Therapy. [Chapters 8-9].

Storm Eunice: House in Brentwood Severely Damaged After 400-Year-Old Tree Brought Down by Strong Winds. (2022 February 19). *Sky News.* Retrieved March 16, 2022, from https://news.sky.com/story/storm-eunice-house-in-brent-wood-severely-damaged-after-400-year-old-tree-brought-down-by-strong-winds-12545879.

Syrian Father Teaches Daughter to Cope with Bombs Through Laughter. (2020, February 18). *Guardianwires.* Retrieved February 28, 2022, from https://www.youtube.com/watch?v=4cvH7aHfE5A.

Tabor, B. (2019). Creating a Mindful Schoolwide Culture to Maximize Learning. In A. Costa & B. Kallick, Eds., *Nurturing Habits of Mind in Early Childhood Classrooms.* ASCD.

Tedeschi, R. G., Moore, B. A., Falke, K., & Goldberg, J. (2020). *Transformed by Trauma: Stories of Posttraumatic Growth.* Boulder: Crest.

Therapists' Tips for Working Through the Stages of Grief. (2020, December 10). *Talkspace.* Retrieved February 28, 2022, from https://www.talkspace.com/blog/stages-of-grief-therapists-advice-grieving/.

Third Stage of Grief: Bargaining. (n.d.). eCondolence.com. Retrieved February 28, 2022, from https://www.econdolence.com/learning-center/grief-and-coping/the-stages-of-grief/third-stage-of-grief-bargaining/.

Trauma: Frozen Moments, Frozen Lives. (2008, July 1). *TheBody.* Retrieved March 1, 2022, from https://www.thebody.com/content/art48754.html.

"Viktor Emil Frankl," (n.d.), Viktor Frankl Institut. Retrieved April 19, 2022, from https://www.univie.ac.at/logotherapy/biography.html.

Vozza, S. (2022, March 10). 5 Subtle Signs You're Headed for Burnout [web log]. Retrieved April 4, 2022, from https://www.fastcompany.com/90727550/5-subtle-signs-youre-headed-for-burnout.

Warning Signs and Risk Factors for Emotional Distress. (n.d.). SAMHSA. Retrieved March 1, 2022, from https://www.samhsa.gov/find-help/disaster-distress-help-line/warning-signs-risk-factors.

What Are the Habits of Mind? (2022, January 19). *TeachThought.* Retrieved April 4, 2022, from https://www.teachthought.com/pedagogy/what-are-the-habits-of-mind.

What Leaders Really Do. (1990) *Harvard Business Review,* 68(3), 103-11. Retrieved March 25, 2022, from https://pubmed.ncbi.nlm.nih.gov/.

"Who Was Viktor Frankl?" (2022), Pursuit of Happiness. *https://www.pursuit-of-happiness.org/history-of-happiness/viktor-frankl/.*

Whorton, L. (2022, March 8). Two Years In, Educators Reflect on Pandemic Leadership. The Holdsworth Center. Retrieved April 4, 2022, from https://holdsworth-center.org/blog/pandemic-leadership-reflections/.

Wilson, D. (2014, May 27). 9 Trigger Warnings for Hamlet. *The Federalist.* Retrieved April 4, 2022, from https://thefederalist.com/2014/05/27/9-trigger-warnings-for-hamlet/.

Wyeth, S. (2014, March 5). Public Speaking Tips: How to Capture and Hold People's Attention. *Inc.com.* Retrieved March 5, 2022, from https://www.inc.com/sims-wyeth/how-to-capture-and-hold-audience-attention.html.

# [ME]PUBLISHING
powered by Meteor Education

Schools are confronting acute issues that attack, distract, and impede education at its core. Shifting learning environments, increased access to information, and the fluidity of student social structures invite schools to think and act differently. METEOR EDUCATION PUBLISHING amplifies the voice of the best thinkers and practitioners who underpin the future of education. We publish content that provides hope and help for those in the daily trenches so that students move from disengaged to engaged learners.

## Great resources from [ME]Pub

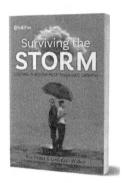

## Amplifying voices to shape the future of education.

*For additional [ME]Pub information and resources visit meb.meteoreducation.com or scan the QR code below.*

# THANK YOU!

UNCHAINED receives a portion of the proceeds from this book to support its heroic efforts in fighting human trafficking.

If you'd like additional information or would like to support UNCHAINED directly, please visit www.unchained-freedom.com.

# UNCHAINED
**A Freedom Alliance**

Made in United States
North Haven, CT
11 June 2022

20111022R00102